RUSSIAN
ARCHITECTURE

RUSSIAN ARCHITECTURE

TRENDS IN NATIONALISM AND MODERNISM

BY

ARTHUR VOYCE

HOOVER INSTITUTE FELLOW IN SLAVIC STUDIES
RUSSIAN ARCHITECTURE

PHILOSOPHICAL LIBRARY

NEW YORK

To R. A. N.

Whose encouragement and help
were of inestimable value.

Author's Acknowledgment

To Dr. Harold H. Fisher, Chairman of the Hoover Institute, and to the staff of the Hoover Library, my sincere thanks for placing so much valuable material at my disposal.

ARTHUR VOYCE

Stanford University

Contents

PART I

THE PRE-REVOLUTIONARY PERIOD

PART II

THE REVOLUTIONARY PERIOD AND CONTEMPORARY SOVIET ARCHITECTURE

vii

List of Illustrations and Maps

PART I

PART II

List of Plates

PART I

PART II

THE ALL-UNION AGRICULTURAL EXPOSITION
1939–1940

References

1. Grabar, I: *Istoria Rouskavo Iskousstva* (*History of Russian Art*), Moscow, 1909. Ed. Knebel.
2. *Sovietskaya Architektura*, (*Soviet architecture*) periodical, Moscow, 1930–31, 1932–33, 1934–46.
3. *Stroitelstvo Moskvy*, (*Moscow Under Construction*), periodical, Moscow, 1933–40.
4. Makowsky, S.: *Talachkino*, Ed. Sodrougestvo, St. Petersburg, 1906.
5. Loukomski, G. K.: *L'Art Decoratif Russe*, V. Freal & Cie., Paris, 1922.
6. Réau, L.: *L'Art Russe*, Henri Laurens Ed., Paris, 1922.
7. Alpatov, M., Brunov, N.: *Geschichte der Altrussischen Kunst*, Dr. Benno Filser Verlag G.M.B.H. Augsburg.
8. Lissistzky, El: *Russland*, Anton Schroll & Co. Wien, 1930.
9. Freeman-Kunitz-Lozowick: *Voices of October*. The Vanguard Press. New York, 1930.
10. Newmarch, R.: *The Russian Arts*. Herbert Jenkins Ltd. London, 1926.
11. Nikolsky, V.: *Istoria Rouskavo Iskousstva* (*History of Russian Art*). R.S.F.S.R. State Pub. House, Berlin, 1923.
12. *Akademia Architekturi* (Academy of Architecture), Organ of the All-Union Academy of Architecture, Moscow.

"For no people can create except in its own subjective image. Hence what people are within, the buildings express without, and, inversely, what the buildings are objectively is a sure index of what the people are subjectively."

LOUIS HENRI SULLIVAN
in "Kindergarten Chats"

"Participation in the endeavor toward human progress does not necessarily imply that every contributing race or people should have an identical viewpoint, similar attitude to every problem, or the same vocabulary for expression. Variety is no impediment to harmony. As a matter of fact, it is one of its essential ingredients. A full and true understanding between all nations—if ever accomplished—can only evolve from an unhampered expression of the genius, the tastes and the specific characteristics of each nation."

VIOLLET LE DUC
"L'art Russe," 1877

Author's Preface

A CRITICAL STUDY of the architecture of any nation is not merely a study of just one phase of its art, but it is an investigation of its very civilization, of its spiritual sources, and of its mental and material make-up. If we would know why certain things are as they are, if we would probe into the psychology of a nation, into its behavioristic pattern, we should look not only to its sociology, politics and economics, but—most important— to the cultural strivings, the artistic aspirations, expressions, and accomplishments of that people.

It has often been asked in recent years—is there such a thing as architectural aesthetics based on Marxian principles? Is there such a thing as Soviet style in architecture? If so, how strongly is it rooted? What are its distinguishing features? What are its relations to modern tendencies in America and Europe? What is its future?

The answer to these questions and an intelligent evaluation of the Soviet concepts of architecture cannot be made without some knowledge of the architecture and the art-aesthetics they seek to supersede.

It seems, therefore, that we must examine not only the recent art currents and tendencies, but look further into the past and investigate the sources which have fed and nourished the countless generations of Russian builders and architects. We must look not only to the Moderns and the Contemporaries but also to the Romantics, the Nationalists of the late 19th Century, the Classics of the early part of that century and, above all, to the "Primitives," to those barely-known building geniuses of ancient and medieval Russia.

It may seem presumptuous to attempt to cover such a large field in so modest a volume, but no claim is hereby made to a final work on the subject. It is realized that this is merely a first attempt and it is only hoped that enough interest will be aroused for further and deeper study of this engrossing theme.

ARTHUR VOYCE

San Francisco

Part I

THE PRE-REVOLUTIONARY ARCHITECTURE

THE CATHEDRAL OF ST. DMITRI
Vladimir, 1194–1197

The Pre-Revolutionary Period

INTRODUCTION

THE PREVAILING MISCONCEPTION about Russian architecture is probably due to the lack of information on the subject, and to the fact that too many of us are prone to rely upon the opinions expressed by certain European historians,[1] who rarely had first-hand knowledge of Russian art.

It is commonly assumed that Russian architecture, up to the time of Peter the Great, is nothing but a barbaric variation of the Greek, Byzantine, Armenian and Persian arts transplanted from their glorious birthplaces to an uncouth wilderness and, therefore, losing all their glamorous qualities and becoming a mere third-rate copy of the original. The architecture of the post-Peter period is considered a mere reflection of the French, Italian or German Baroque. As to the recent architecture of the post-Revolutionary period, it is either dismissed altogether as nothing but utilitarian engineering, or regarded as an imitation of the modern Western European architecture.

These beliefs are mostly based on the premise that from the very early days of Russian history clear up to the nineteenth century, Russia had always relied upon foreign experts in the management of her governmental, military, civil and in-

[1] NOTE: The famous work of Viollet-le-Duc, "L'art Russe" (1877), which for many years was considered the authoritative work on Russian architecture, is based entirely on descriptions and drawings sent to him by his Moscow friends. He, himself, never visited Russia.

dustrial institutions. The legend persists that the Varangians were invited to rule her, the Greeks to give her religion, and later on German, Italian, French and Dutch experts in various lines were asked to help in the transformation of this backward country into a modern European state. It is naturally easy to come to the conclusion that the art of Russia is also of an imported, hybrid character. Historians point to a few architectural oddities, as for example, to the Church of Basil the Blessed in Moscow,* to this aptly called "garden of monstrous vegetables," as a striking example of "pure Russian" art.

It is, of course, true that the intellectual and commercial contacts between Russia and her neighbors, to the South and West, have had a continual influence on Russian art. But any serious student of Russia will quickly discover that the history of her art is not only that of borrowing and of outright adoption, but of assimilation and reincarnation of foreign art forms into her own forms, stamped with her own national genius.

Much of the cultural and artistic wealth of Europe and Asia had been transplanted into Russia, but in the words of Professor Malkiel Jirmounsky (of the University of Paris), "her peculiar national mentality, her rich imagination transformed and resolved these diverse elements into an ensemble altogether homogeneous." Professor Jirmounsky characterizes the qualities of the Russian artistic genius in the following words: "Russian art manifests a rare force in absorbing and assimilating elements from without, though opposite in their character, transfiguring them into a national substance." [1] The historian of Russian art, Igor Grabar, in discussing the origin and evolution of her architecture, points to another characteristic of Russian culture: "With all her visible poverty in

* Plates XVII, XIX.
[1] Gazette des Beaux Arts, Paris, March 1931.

comparison with foreign cultures, there is hidden in her an enormous power of magnetism and attraction, which had many a time caused the assimilation and thorough Russification of the best representatives of the strongest cultures of Europe." [2]

THE ANTECEDENTS OF RUSSIAN ARCHITECTURE

Russian architecture had its genesis in two very different and characteristically opposite sources: Byzantine and Northern, the latter having ancient connections with the old Nordic art. Greeks and Transcaucasians were the first architects of southern Russia. They built at Kiev and Tchernigov, or if they themselves did not actually do the planning, the edifices were influenced by Byzantine art. But even in these provinces, though in close proximity to Byzantium, there soon appeared characteristic departures from the pure Byzantine forms. These departures were even more marked in the Novgorod and Pskov provinces, farther removed from Byzantium. Instead of producing servile copies, Medieval Russian architecture created something very different. The interest of this art resides chiefly in the partial or complete transformations imposed by the Russian national genius upon the forms imported into a new milieu.

Other numerous influences, Persian and Hindu, had arrived rapidly to add themselves and even to contradict the Byzantine influence. These various foreign importations were also quickly absorbed, digested and assimilated into the Russian body artistic; they were modified and interwoven with the local Russian traditional art forms, and thus a national art had been created.

At the beginning of the twelfth century two types of archi-

[2] History of Russian Art by Igor Grabar, Moscow (1909).

tecture could be distinguished. One was that of southern and central Russia, where the original forms influenced by the Byzantine elements and subsequently by the Western elements, culminated in combining the characteristics of Byzantine and Romanesque arts. The other was that of the more politically and artistically independent republics of northern Russia. The modest and rational tastes of the republican bourgeoisie, the exigencies of the severe climate and the influence of the neighboring Germanic cities, Riga and Revel, had paved the way for the liberation of the native architecture from the older influences of Byzantium and had created an entirely distinct architecture.

The first cathedrals, the first churches of Kiev and Tchernigov were a mixture of forms and influences: the vaults constructed in stone were inspired by Byzantium, but the plan of the churches conformed to the type created by the Greek Christians of Transcaucasia. The mosaics are pure Greek in outline but quite original in coloring.

In the churches of Vladimir and Souzdal provinces there are apparent the characteristic manifestations of Romanesque architecture. Persia and India had also contributed to the lacelike decorations covering the walls; lions, tigers, palms and all the other attributes of the far East and central Asia are found on these walls. Outstanding examples are .the Church of the Intercession on the Nerl near Vladimir (1165) and the Cathedral of St. Dmitri at Vladimir (1195).*

The typical scheme of the buildings in the North was as follows: a cube with one or three salient portions of semicylindrical shape on the east front, which corresponds to the altar or altars within the church, and four massive piers carrying the cupola on arches and pendentives. The cupolas are of a more oval shape than those of the Byzantine churches.

* Plates IX–XII.

They resemble in outline the forms of the ancient helmets and are better adapted to the heavy snowfalls and rains of the northern climates, the flatter shapes of the original cupolas having been found impracticable. (This is the origin of the more or less pointed cupolas which prevail among the churches of the north.) For the same reason, the Byzantine flat roofs were replaced by steep intersecting gable roofs, and the generous windows of Constantinople by small narrow chinks in the wall. These simple white, rather squat, cube-shaped churches with their enormous blue and gold helmet-cupolas are strikingly beautiful in the setting of the sombre, lake-dotted landscape.

In the sixteenth century Moscow led the way in the substitution of the traditional Byzantine cupola (glava) by the "tent-shaped" pyramid (shater). The late Pskovian method of supporting the cupola on arches receding "in steps" (kokoshniki) instead of on columns and pendentives, was adopted and further perfected into a new treatment of the penetrating arch. It was made a prominent feature in the general scheme. By means of these tapering-off arches, arranged in tiers, the square or the polygon of the base led up to the superimposed octagon crowned by a pyramidal tower on which was usually mounted a lantern. The tiers of arches (kokoshniki), the "tent-shaped" (shater) roofs, the polygonal forms of the bases are all, undoubtedly, derived from the forms of the wood architecture of the North. The outstanding examples of this type are the stone Churches of the Ascension at Kolomenskoe (1532)* and of the Transfiguration at Ostrovo (1550), both of these near Moscow. The pyramidal "tent-shaped" forms of the roof, whose character is distinctly racial, took the place of the alien cupola. The development of these nationally beloved forms was unfortunately cut short

* Plates XV, XVI

by an edict of the clergy (1650) in the belief that only the
sacrosanct pentacupolar form (piatiglavie) was fit for the
Greek Catholic Church. It is significant that in the provinces
far away from the watchful eye of the upper clergy the people
obstinately stuck to the "tent-shaped" pyramidal forms and
built their churches as of old.

Under the influence of the Orient the architecture of the
Moscow region became more elaborate and more richly ornamented. Over the intimately-Russian structural forms were
lavishly spread the decorative motifs borrowed from the Near
and Far East. Generally, chiseled brick was used to cover the
wall surfaces of the churches, and a great decorative quality
was derived from this material. There was also a profuse use
of vari-colored materials which produced brilliant results.
Another favorite method of ornamentation was the employment of polychrome friezes of bird motifs girdling the building, and bands of faïence, painted ornamentation and symbolic figures were lavishly used. The foreign ornamental
forms were nearly always amalgamated with the ornament
of geometric character of Old Russia.

THE EARLY ITALIAN RENAISSANCE AND THE BAROQUE
INFLUENCES IN MUSCOVY

Moscow, the capital of Muscovy of ancient Russia, absorbed all the artistic aspirations and realizations of Russia beginning with the end of the fourteenth century, when Vladimir
and Souzdal were eliminated from the political field. With the
fall of Constantinople in 1453 Moscow became the metropolis
of the East. Ivan III (1462–1505) had delivered Russia from
the yoke of the Tartars, but the evil effects of the Mongol
invasion on Russian life and its building art lingered on for

quite a while. Russian craftsmen, as a direct result of the long subjugation to the Mongols, had almost forgotten the art of masonry building. Many a church begun in the reign of Ivan III had its walls crumble even before its completion. The czar had to import foreign architectural talent for carrying out of his building projects.

It is not quite known why Ivan III should have invited Italian instead of French masters. Whether that was a mere coincidence, or whether the great Czar felt that there was a closer kinship of spirit and taste between him and the Italians, the fact was that Fioraventi, the Bolognese, and Solario, the Milanese, and a number of others were invited. The Italian masters, naturally introduced the architectural forms of their native land, and so it came about that the churches of Lucca and Pisa, have their counterpart in Moscow. The Kremlin in Moscow, this Russian acropolis, which so many consider as the quintessence of Russo-Asiatic art, is in reality, the creation of the Moscow colony of Italian architects of the Renaissance.

It must be emphasized though that the Italian masters did not always have a free hand. Their architectural activities, at the suggestion and sometimes at the insistence of the Russians, were circumscribed by the Byzantine traditions expressed in so many of the monuments of Russian antiquity. The Russians evidently could not quite relinquish the hallowed older forms that had become classic to them.

The great debt that Russia owes to the Italian masters is that the latter introduced a better, perfected technique of construction. They taught the Russians to make better bricks, to make a mortar with stronger binding qualities; they taught them to fill up the inner wall spaces not with loose gravel and sand but with bricks and cement, and to reinforce walls and vaults, not with wood, but with iron, etc. They have also enriched the Russian ornamental vocabulary with Renaissance motifs.

It was only when the Russians had mastered the building technique that they could give a freer rein to their artistic imagination. The period extending from the second half of the sixteenth century, clear through the seventeenth century, was the golden era in the history of Russian architecture. Moscow had become the center of Russian art. The invitation of the Italian architects to Moscow in 1475 served merely as an incentive that quickened the Russian reaction to the traditions of Byzantine art—a fact which made Russian architecture more self-confident and self-sufficient.

The new found technical knowledge and better methods of construction borrowed from the Italians, combined with the influence of the Byzantine art-elements incorporated in so many of the cathedrals and churches, and above all the forms inherent in their own native wooden architecture, were the principal factors in the evolution of that very individual and richly fanciful architecture known as the "Moscow Style" of the seventeenth century. The Byzantine traditions having held sway for several centuries became weaker and weaker in their influence, gradually dissolved and finally crystallized into a new artistic style. By the end of the seventeenth century there was hardly anything in common between the architectures of Muscovy and Byzantium. The decisive factors in the formation of the new style were the forms evolved from the architecture of the Russian North.

The Renaissance period, at its height, had missed Russia altogether. It had affected Russian architecture mainly at the time of its very early and very late (Baroque) phases. The first phase of the Renaissance had left but a slight trace on some of the architectural details. It reflected itself mainly in the methods of construction technique. It hardly touched the building forms then strongly in favor. On the other hand, the phase of the Renaissance called the Baroque had an enormous influence and had caused the creation and perfection of entirely new building types. Russia at the end of the seventeenth century had accepted the idioms of the then prevailing style, but it had re-fashioned them into types entirely individual to Russia. One reason was that the Baroque in Moscow was not the result of a normal growth and gradual development of the various phases of the Renaissance but because it had appeared on the scene suddenly. Another reason was that Moscow did not receive the motifs of that style in their pure form directly from the West, but from the Ukraine, which in turn received them from Poland and Lithuania. In a little over twenty-five years this style had developed, had grown to maturity and had achieved a finish and that distinct Russian flavor which is still the marvel and pride of Muscovy. The best example of that period is the Church of the Holy Virgin in Fili near Moscow (1693).*

THE PETERSBURGIAN PHASES OF THE BAROQUE AND THE ADVENT OF CLASSICISM

With Peter the Great began a new era in Russian history and at the same time in Russian art and architecture. Russia was gradually emerging from her centuries-long seclusion. The great Czar's reforms had sharpened the division between the upper and the lower classes and thus had destroyed the most remarkable characteristics that distinguished the pre-Peter period of Russia's art history. The homogeneity of her civilization and the union that existed between her people and her art were broken. The essentially religious art of the

* Plates XXIV–XXXIII.

pre-Peter period gave way to lay art. The language of the earlier architects and the Icon painters that could be understood equally well by the great nobleman or the simple moujik was superseded by an exclusive alien tongue. The new art imported from the West could appeal only to a very limited number of the upper stratum of an Europeanized nobility, a class which had lost all contact with the people, and had become contemptuous of the art and even thé language of the people. We thus see the creation of a condition where the art of the people was allowed to vegetate in the villages while the art cultivated by the aristocracy took the front of the stage.

It was Peter's desire that his new capital (founded in 1703) should symbolize the advent of the new era, that it should be the Russian "window" towards the West. St. Petersburg, therefore, was to be laid out and built along the lines of a great Occidental capital. Its architecture had to be up to date and authentically European. It had to be as different as possible from the old metropolis which symbolized Old Mother Russia, and which the plebeian classes still considered their capital. Peter, therefore, set out (circa 1713) to engage European architects, artists, and engineers wherever he could find them. Unfortunately, most of the people he engaged, with the exception of the Frenchman, Leblond, and the Italian, Trezzini, were second and third raters. There were many Dutch, German, Italian and French architects and craftsmen. All of them had arrived practically simultaneously. Because of the urgency many of them had to work side by side very often on adjoining buildings. Each one of them, naturally, contributed his own racial and national characteristics. It was even a common occurrence for a single building to have been designed by an Italian, started by a German, continued by a Frenchman, followed up by another Italian, with the possible interference of still another German or Dutchman. It is easy to imagine what sort of an "architectural unity" could be achieved through this unique collective creative process. It was thus that much that was inferior and unworthy in architecture invaded the new capital. The foreign masters and their Russian pupils were all under the spell of the international character of the then predominant Baroque but each one of them interpreted it in the manner of his native land. St. Petersburg had thus acquired a physiognomy all its own. In Peter's time it was, indeed, a strange jumble of Dutch, German, French and Italian Baroque with hardly a trace of Russian character or flavor.

It was only in the course of time, when numbers of Russians and Russian-born children of the foreign-colony architects returned to Russia from their architectural studies abroad, that the quality of architecture rose. Along with an improved construction technique these youngsters brought back with them a new appreciation for the architecture of their mother country. Rastrelli (1700–1770) who studied and traveled extensively abroad, is a fine example of that group. He, the Russian-born son of a Parisian emigré sculptor, created an entire architectural epoch in Russia. His project, especially his model for the Smolney Convent, clearly shows that the inspiration for this work is drawn from old Russian sources. This fairy-like monastery is truly a product of the Russian genius. The whole naive, toy-like composition is permeated with the national spirit (Plates XL–XLII).

Rastrelli's numerous pupils spread his ideas to the far corners of Russia, but in St. Petersburg, as indeed much earlier, in the West, the signs presaging a discontent with all Baroque forms were beginning to be apparent. The ever growing floridness of those forms was becoming very tiresome. The ornate decadent Baroque gave way to the re-discovered charm of classic antiquity. Prince Shuvalov in planning for the creation of the Russian Academy of Fine Arts (the middle of the eighteenth century) turned for help and advice not to Rastrelli, but to Kokorinov, and the Frenchman, de la Mothe, the exponents of purity of style. Their "Transition Style" was superseded by the more classic tendencies of the style of Louis XVI. Architecture from then on, seemed to be going back into the past with terrific speed, immersing itself into antiquity. Inspiration was sought in the study of the early masters of the Renaissance, of ancient Rome, Greece and their colonies.

The love held by Catherine the Great for the civilization and monuments of classic Rome, coupled with a passion for building, gave rise to a great architectural activity. Palaces, buildings for the housing of government institutions, hospitals, private villas and residences with which she rewarded her innumerable "favorites" and faithful coworkers sprang up in and about the capital. Her ambition to create a great metropolis, a veritable "Northern Palmyre" was soon realized. The inspiration for these buildings was drawn mainly from the forms of the architecture of Rome. One of the great geniuses of that epoch was the Russian architect Starov (1743–1808), the builder of the Tauride Palace. This building, remodeled so many times, was destined a century and a quarter later to house the ill-fated Douma. Its beautiful, grandiose colonnade had become a favorite model to be admired and copied. It soon had become a feature of many palaces and private residences. From the Russian capital it was transferred to the provinces and it soon blossomed out in many of the great seigneurial manors, the "nests of the nobles" all over Russia. This patrician Roman architectural feature transferred from the hills of Rome to the banks of the Dnieper and the Dniester does not seem incongruous at all. On the contrary, it fitted itself admirably into its new surroundings and merged harmoniously with the green and white of their birch trees and the gentle slopes of their hills and dales, so much so, that it had become a part of the national substance and a harmonious feature of the Russian rural landscape.

The Classicism of Catherine the Great was followed by the Classicism of Alexander I. The infatuation for things Roman gave way to the worship of archaic Greece of the fifth and sixth centuries B.C. The trend of those times was away from the magnificence and splendor of the Roman-Ionic and Corinthian colonnades of the Catherine epoch. The architectural pendulum swung farther towards the severe simplicity of the Greek Doric order, toward smooth unbroken wall surfaces, to be punctuated only for emphasis with perhaps a sculptured frieze or a light ornamental figure, suggesting the structural elements of the building frame, simple in itself, and the logical outgrowth of the plan.

This was a feature which was very much akin to the architectural traditions distinguishing the Novgorod and the Pskov periods. Though there was a distance of five centuries between these epochs yet there was a surprising similarity in the ideals that dominated them. While the European enthusiasm for archaic Greece was only a short-lived one, having been superseded by new attractions, in Russia it had rooted itself deep into the soil, and judging by evidences, into a very favorable and fertile soil. The classic revival contributed much to the secular work of Russia of that period. It caused a flowering of architecture such as Russia had not known since the days of Novgorod. *Strange as it may seem, its echo, as we shall see, was to be heard almost exactly a century later under very different circumstances, motivated by entirely new incentives.*

A great deal of credit for the quality of that work must be given to Alexander I. He was one of the very few Russian autocrats, who exercised a beneficial influence upon his country's architecture. He evidently inherited the passion for building from his grandmother, the great Catherine, but fortunately, he was less given to the capricious self-indulgences which are exhibited here and there in the luxuriant outbursts of this glamorous lady's imagination. A catholic taste, a keen sense of the beautiful and, above all, tact were a part of the make up of this "Arbiter Elegantiarum," qualities which made his co-workers, especially in the first part of his reign, accept his ideas on civic planning and building without the feeling that these were being forced upon them. The result was a great disciplined and harmonious unity in his building program. Modern St. Petersburg (present Leningrad) owes its finer aspects to him. More than half of it was erected during his reign, with his direct assistance.

THE BIRTH OF THE "GENUINE RUSSIAN" SCHOOL

Unfortunately this Alexandrian period was to be of only short duration. The storm that had broken loose in Europe during the Napoleonic Wars had brought in its wake the spirit of Nationalism. The Romantic movement was born, and it had infected all of Europe. For the new post-war generation the forms of the antique world of Greece were too severe, too cold and soulless. It wanted more warmth, more comfort, more "gemütlichkeit" and therefore, the search was on for new forms. Simultaneously with the fall of Bonaparte, there awoke the instinct of national self-discovery, a search for racial inheritances. The nations had turned from the far-off alien Greek world to the things bequeathed to them by their own fathers. They had turned to the study and the revival of the Gothic, a style comparatively free from the influences of the antique world.

One would have assumed that the Russian architects would also have turned to the study of their own national architectural inheritance, examples of which abounded in Novgorod, Pskov and Moscow. Nothing could be farther from what actually happened. They, too, succumbed to the infatuation for the Gothic style. Alas, there was never to be a Russian Gothic. The soul of the Russian architect was evidently barren of the qualities and impulses that gave expression to this noble style in northern France and England. The efforts of the Russian imitators of the Gothic were a dismal failure. One of the principal factors in that failure was the all-stifling, spirit-crushing atmosphere that prevailed during the reign of Nicholas I. Unlike the benevolent and cultivated Alexander I, Nicholas was a martinet, a hard, unbending, narrow-minded autocrat. Not only the motto, "L' etat c'est moi," but "L'art c'est moi" could be well attributed to him. He actually issued a decree in which he forbade the erection of any church or public building in Russia unless it was in the style approved by the "all highest." There was to be no dabbling in anything that might conceivably interfere with the official conception of art in his state.

The canons of this style, the only one suitable for the Greek orthodox church, the only "Genuine Russian" style were, paradoxically enough, developed and formulated by the German architect, Thon, the author of the Church of St. Catherine on Peterhof Road. This church proved to be the forerunner of the era of coarseness and vulgarity in architectural taste; it served as a model for hundreds of others, all designed in the 1830's in this, so called, "Russian" style. Other architects, most of them foreigners, be it noted, adopted this official style. The Englishman Sherwood took the Church of Vasilyi Blajenny (Basil the Blessed) as his inspiration for the construction of the Historical Museum in Moscow.* Indeed, one can find in this building all the details that characterize its famous prototype: the outside covered stairways, the paunchy columns, the hanging arch keystones, the overlapping "kokoshniki." In a word he missed nothing of the "local color." There may have been some excuse for that as the two buildings face each other on the Red Square in Moscow. A much less excusable example of this pseudo-Russian style is the Church of the Resurrection in Petersburg built by Parland (Russian born, but of Scotch descent). Looming up but a few feet from the Corinthian peristyle of Rossi,[1] the ribbed and imbricated onion-shaped cupolas of this church are altogether out of harmony with the Baroque and Empire architecture of the surroundings.

This official "Russian" style, imposed from on high, developed into a stilted version of the national motifs. It became identified with ginger bread details, filigree coxcombs, carved "tassels" and "towels," presumably derived from the rustic art of the village. Its originator was Ropet (whence the name "Ropet Style") and its patron and advocate was Stassov. It found favor with the affluent merchants and the parvenu industrialists and became the raging fashion for town houses, suburban villas and "datchas." The spirit of this "style" has unfortunately survived clear to the days of the

[1] Carlo di Giovanni Rossi (1775–1849). The last representative of the Empire style in Russia. He built the Alexander Theatre, the Palace of the Senate, the War Office, etc.
* Plate LXVI.

beginning of the Revolution. It had begun to show some promisingly sane features only in the last decades of the nineteenth century, when a few truly talented architects revolted against this pseudo-Russian style and started a movement for the revival of the ancient Novgorod and Pskov traditions, seeking inspiration in the simplicity and purity of those art-forms for their own work.

Among the precursors of the coming era of better taste was the gifted architect Victor Hartman (1854–1873). His heroic project for a gateway into the city of Kiev (never built) and his fantastic but interesting building for the printing establishment of Mamontov in Moscow (1872) were a bold attempt to revive the spirit of the old Russian timber architecture.[1] Nikonov's house for the Bassin family in Petersburg and Bogdanov's wooden churches and charming private residences, in and about Petersburg and Moscow, are all outstanding examples of the so-called "Russian Renaissance."

One might characterize the last few pre-Revolutionary decades in the history of Russian art as a period of struggle between two mighty forces, between nationalistic Slavophil and cosmopolitan European tendencies. The Nationalistic movement begun by Ropet, having taken on a sturdier and healthier aspect, under the guidance of a saner Nationalist school was offering a strong resistance to the various phases of European Modernistic currents in art and architecture. It had won in architecture, though not so decisive a victory as it had won in the other arts. Russian motifs in building and decoration became as general as the folksong themes in symphonic music.

[1] Moussorgsky, one of the "mighty five" in the Nationalist group of composers, inspired by the drawings and the water colors of Hartman translated a series of them into music; under the title: "Pictures from an Exhibition."

SLAVOPHILISM VS. OCCIDENTALISM IN ARCHITECTURE

With the emancipation of the serfs and the general liberal changes in the social order during the reign of Alexander II, Russian art and letters were stimulated by new vital forces. The semi-feudal order was fast crumbling away and Industrialism and Capitalism were rapidly taking its place. The growth of Russian Industrialism, in the last part of the nineteenth century, had strengthened the influence and accentuated the importance of the Russian middle classes. It was only natural that the rising bourgeoisie should make a tremendous effort to free itself from inherited cramping traditions, from religious superstitions and from the formalism of the entrenched political castes. The idea of personal and social liberties, naturally, had to be reflected in the art of that period and hence the great vogue of the new iconoclastic tendencies in art. "Style Moderne," "Art Nouveau," and later on, the "Viennese Secession" became the fashion. The new movement, running true to form, initiated a downright anarchy in the architectural esthetic, emphasizing an intentional break with all tradition, with everything that was recognized universally showing a pronounced contempt for all logic and reason. Cheap exoticism and esthetic license became the ruling forces of the moment with the result that irrationalism in building, queerness in detail, and lack of the most elementary comfort in interior furnishings became rampant in Russian architecture and applied arts.

With the growth of individualism the urge of an intimate personal ideal of beauty grew all the stronger. A desire to express the new-found liberty and a desire for intimacy were the principal factors in the search for new stylistic expressions. The most important element, whose influence super-

imposed itself upon the literature, music, painting and architecture of that period in a very marked way, was the spirit
of the race, the national element.

In the life of Russia there have always been periods of
strong foreign influences, only to be digested and assimilated
by the ever hovering phantoms of her past. The creative
artistic genius of the nation, in the words of S. Makowsky,[1]
had gone back, again and again, to the distant past, and the
new forms became saturated with its charm. The latent forces
of her national antiquity always affected the creative consciousness of the new epoch. Russia, for more than one reason,
had conserved its national distinction. In spite of the abyss
that separated its aristocracy from the lower classes, cultivated Russian art, because of its intimate impulses, was much
closer to the popular rustic art than was the case in Western
Europe. Because of a long isolation from the rest of Europe
and her artistic influences, the art of the people was strong
enough to influence and modify the new stylistic tendencies
in their aspirations for a new expression. The Russian exponents of this new art, in looking about for new forms, had
turned to national motifs and to the primitive sources of
Russian culture. This new school had tried, at the end of the
nineteenth century, to turn the hands of time back to the
style of the epoch before Peter the Great, towards the models
of the village "Koustar" industries, the poesy of national antiquity and the art of the people.

It was the hope of the Slavophils that Russian culture and
Russian art would develop along entirely national lines. Their
premise was that, unlike the West, with its rationalism and
personal freedom, ancient Russia lived by religious faith and

[1] "Talachkino" by S. Makowsky, published by "Sodrougestvo," Moscow,
1908.

community interests, and therefore, Russian history must obey a different set of laws; and that the forms of her life, of her growth and of her art were subject to a special destiny. Their conception of a new expression in architecture was a style grounded in the purely racial patrimony. Their envisioned heaven was a purely indigenous Russian Christian paradise. According to them the truly artistic sources, were not the ungodly, international ideas of the European modernists, not the city with its destructive forces, with its commercialism, its factories and its revolutionary proletariat, but the village with its patriarchal traditions, the Christian humility of the old peasant.

It is curious and rather piquant, as L. Reau points out, that this Muscovite Nationalism was "made in Germany." [1] Smoldering for centuries, and flaring up every now and then under the impetus of external and internal stresses,[2] this movement crystallized into a definite credo with the publication of the Hegelian social philosophic theories (about the middle of the nineteenth century). The father of the Nazi movement in Germany became unwittingly the apostle of Slavophilism, and the "Chosen People's" doctrine, reserved *exclusively* for the Germans was enthusiastically taken up by the Slavophils and applied to the Russians. As is usually the case with such movements Slavophilism went to ridiculous excesses. It degenerated into a sort of a naive and noisy chauvinism. It, however, did have its beneficial effects. Thanks to this movement, Russia recovered its national consciousness which was almost obliterated by a transplanted cosmopolitanism. This vogue opened up new vistas for original creative thought.

[1] Louis Réau, "L'Art Russe" Henri Laurens, Editeur, Paris, 1922.
[2] The troubled times of 1612, the revolt against the reforms of Peter the Great, the War of 1812, etc.

The Nationalists were seeking to revive the ancient traditions of Russian art and architecture and to put new life into the old forms by infusing them with the freshness, simplicity and the fantastic picturesqueness of the rustic Russian. It was because of this movement that the direction and the quality of the art of the city began to be seriously influenced by the primitive rural art, an art that had been developing through many centuries in the isolated quietness of the village and in the calm of the limitless steppes and forests. On the eve of the great events of our days, Russia turned its eyes towards a distant past. Artists like Nesterov, Vasnetzov and Repin probed into the artistic character of Russian antiquity; they searched for, and studied the costumes, brocades, the wood-carvings, the gaily colored "terems" and churches with their golden cupolas. They unearthed whole strata of forgotten things, and saturated themselves with the charm and poetry of the past. They discovered the colorful originality of "Wooden Russia," the antique frescoes, and the bizarre flowery designs and decorations on the walls of the old monasteries, all the splendor of a vanished epoch, all that was created during the long dark barbaric age of Russian history.

Towards the very end of the nineteenth century the Russian national art sentiment lost its potency. The new generation realized that the narrow formulas of the Nationalists were as lacking in life as the vapid cliches of the Academy. A new group was formed, rallying around the art magazine "Mir Iskousstva." [1] Though outspoken individualists they too hoped to further the cause of the national art, but their Nationalism was of a much less narrow and of a less aggressive type. It was

[1] Mir Iskousstva (The World of Art) founded in 1899, edited by A. Benois and S. Diaguilev.

an artistic movement not limited exclusively to the revival of the Moscow traditions of the pre-Peter period. It had found in the post-Peter period many things worthy of study and admiration. In architecture, as in the other arts, it took the form of a sharp reaction to the pseudo-Russian style. Architects like Shchouko and Fomin at Petersburg, Joltovsky at Moscow, were the leaders in the revival of the Palladian Classicism of the eighteenth century—the Rococo of the Tzarina Elizabeth period, and the "Empire" style of Alexander I, while Malioutin and his co-workers at Talachkino carried on their work in the rustic manner of rural Russia. The artists, Roerich, Bilibin and Stelletzky have delved further into the study of archaic Russia. Benois and Bakst, the great decorative and scenic artists, have carried on their work in the opera and ballet productions of Diaguilev and have done much in introducing to Europe and America the many phases and moods of Russia's art in its "holiday attire."

Nikolai Roerich (1874–   ), with his valuable studies of old Russian architecture, revived the robust pictorial and architectural idioms of archaic Russia. He made the old semilegendary world of Russia, the world of the Norsemen and the Varangians, live again before our eyes. Ivan Bilibin, another archaist, made a thorough study of old Icons, miniatures and, above all, the Byzantine sources of Russian art and the popular rustic, colored prints (loubki). His stage-setting for "Boris Godunov" and his highly imaginative illustrations of Russian fairy tales are well known in this country.

Leon Bakst, with his Semitic temperament, was attracted by the Oriental undercurrents in Russian art. Though his art is not limited to any period or country, it is essentially permeated with the spirit of Russia. In his stage-settings and costumes for the Russian ballets and operas he did much to acquaint and startle Europe, America, and the Russians themselves with the dazzling and Slavically sensuous quality of his art.

Sergey Malioutin working at the Talachkino School [1] yields to the almost primitive fantasy and local color of the Volga region. His wooden Teremok, his Chalet-theatre at Talachkino are fine examples of that mode,—they are fairy-like, ingenious and intimately Russian. The bizarre interior decorations are inspired by the carved and sculptured prows of the Volga boats. His furniture and balalaika designs, though lacking in elementary logic and utility, make up in picturesqueness and national flavor.

These are but a few of the artists and architects, who have not merely resurrected and enriched the artistic traditions of old and rural Russia, but who have taught the outside world and their own people to see, through the eyes of the past generations, Mother Russia,—a more alluring, a more fantastic, though at times, a more strange and terrifying land.

The efforts and rising hopes of those yearning Retrospectivists were not to be realized. They were to be submerged by stronger currents of life. Dreams of beautiful excursions into an archaic past, into a land of fairy tales, and into the age of Catherine and Alexander were indeed delightful. Those narrators of the stories of Russia's childhood and adolescent days were gifted story tellers. The only trouble was that they failed to notice the rapidly changing social and economic currents. After all, it was a far cry from the wooden, naive, toy-like architecture of the old Russian "Izbas," from the "terems" of medieval-Russia's boyars, or the imitation-Versailles palaces of the Grand Dukes, to the needs of the new

[1] Talachkino School for Peasant-Crafts and Decorative Arts (near Smolensk) under the patronage of Princess Tenicheva, an artist of renown herself.

age, the rising generation of modern princes of commerce and captains of industry.

The art of Russia, faithfully mirroring her civilization, reflected the frailty of the Russian social structure. This edifice tumbled over (even as the Russian fairy tale huts, supported on chick legs) as soon as its props (Absolutism) were knocked out. The chasm that separated her ruling class from the masses was never bridged over in spite of the efforts of her Nationalists. It had contributed not a little to the duality of her civilization and to the creation of conflicting elements within her art.

THE BYZANTINE PERIOD

XI–XVI Centuries

PLATE I

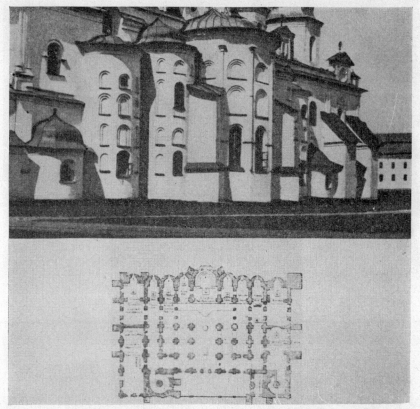

"History of Russian Architecture," Igor Grabar

THE CATHEDRAL OF SAINT SOPHIA

Plan and East elevation showing the oldest altar part of the Cathedral

The Cathedral, founded by Prince Iaroslav, The Wise, in 1036, is one of the greatest monuments of Russian antiquity. In its early days it was the center of the Kiev Kremlin overlooking the Dnieper. In its present state the cathedral is the result of many additions (especially to the South and North sides) and cardinal alterations.

It was damaged considerably during the Second World War.

PLATE II   THE CATHEDRAL OF SAINT SOPHIA

PLATE III

THE CATHEDRAL OF SAINT SOPHIA
General view, Kiev, 1036

PLATE IV   *Courtesy Sovfoto, N.Y.*

THE CATHEDRAL OF THE ASSUMPTION

The Pechersk Lavra, "The Monastery of the Catacombs," Kiev, 1073–1089

A monastery ensemble built over ancient "Varangian" caves in the old Kiev district known as Pechersk (the district of caves). Many relics of the early Russian Saints were preserved in those caves and the monastery had been a pilgrimage shrine ever since its foundation by Saints Anthony and Theodosius. (The monastery is in ruins as a result of the Second World War.)

PLATE V

CHURCH OF THE SAVIOUR
Nereditza near Novgorod, 1198
South West elevation

The little Church of the Transfiguration of the Saviour—destroyed during World War II—was one of the early, most charming examples of the Novgorod Type of architecture. It was renowned for its cycle of frescoes done at the end of the 12th century. They were the most celebrated survivals of ancient Russian painting.

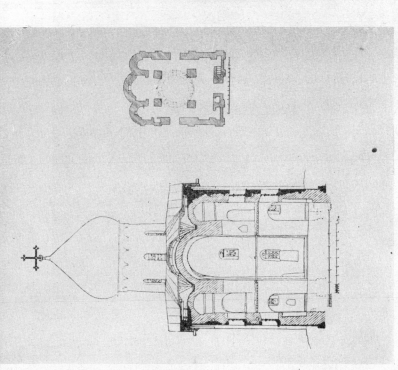

CHURCH OF THE SAVIOUR
Nereditza near Novgorod, 1198
Plan and Section; Measured Drawing by Pokrishkin

PLATE VI

CHURCH OF THE SAVIOUR AT KOVALEVO

Novgorod, 1345

A small structure of great simplicity and charm; one of the best examples of the Novgorod transitional period, tending toward ... size in the number and size of the apses, modification in the form of the cupola and introduction of

PLATE VII

CHURCH OF ST. PETER AND PAUL
Novgorod, 1406

Detail of apse, showing exterior arcading and the decorative band under the eave.

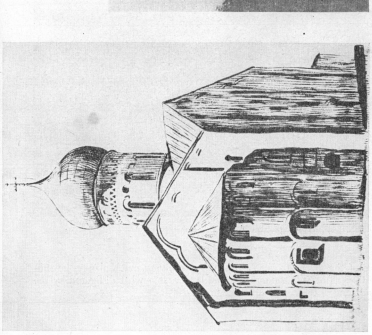

CHURCH OF SAINT THEODORE STRATILAT
Novgorod, 1360

Square in plan with only one semi-circular apse. Note the steep intersecting gables and the helmet (shlem) shaped cupola, features best adapted to the northern climate.

PLATE VIII

CHURCH OF THE 12 APOSTLES
Novgorod, 1455

Originally one of the loveliest churches of Novgorod, very much akin in its simplicity to the Church of St. Theodore Stratilat. Later, somewhat disfigured by the tasteless remodelling of the cupola after the fire of 1904.

PLATE IX

THE CATHEDRAL OF THE ASSUMPTION
Vladimir, 1158–1189

One of the best known examples of Ecclesiastical architecture of the 12th century, greatly revered as one of the sacred monuments of early Russian history. It served as a model for the Cathedral of the Assumption in Moscow, built by Fioravanti the Bolognese in 1475, at the behest of Ivan III (the Great).

PLATE X

Photo, I. Grabar

CHURCH OF THE INTERCESSION OF THE HOLY VIRGIN
on the River Nerl near Vladimir, circa 1165

Built by Prince Andrey Bogolubski of white sandstone, the church is one of the outstanding examples of the Vladimir style. It is well preserved and remains one of the finest expressions of the national genius.

It is rectangular in plan. Three semi-circular apses project from the eastern end. Blind ornamental arcades run around the top, and ever-so-often the engaged slender columns run clear to the ground. The other sides, vertically divided into three panels, are also decorated with arcades just below the narrow windows. The portals are deeply recessed and richly decorated.

PLATE XI

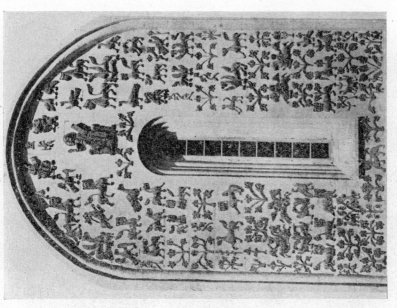

THE CATHEDRAL OF ST. DMITRI
Vladimir, 1194–1197

Detail of south side. The "King David" panel, embroidered with elaborate low-relief sculpture of symbolic figures, fantastic creatures and conventionalized tree and vegetable forms.

Photo, I. Grabar

THE CATHEDRAL OF ST. DMITRI
Vladimir, 1194–1197

The best preserved and most elaborately decorated example of the Vladimir-Suzdal churches built prior to the Tartar invasion.

PLATE XII

THE CATHEDRAL OF ST. DMITRI

Vladimir, 1194–1197

Detail showing the helmet type dome (or cupola), the carved stone ornamentation of the drum and a fragment of the decorative arcade, encircling the upper part of the apses.

PLATE XIII

THE CATHEDRAL OF ST. GEORGE

Yuriev Polski, 1230–1234

Fragment of south wall decorative sculpture in low-relief. Note the stylized forms of the Saint, the griffin and the Sirin (the fabulous creature with the body of a bird and the head of a man, one of the oldest decorative motifs of Russian art).

PLATE XIV

THE CHURCH IN THE CONVENT OF SAMTAVIS, GEORGIA

Transcaucasia, 14th century

An example of the late Georgian style. The exterior is distinguished by the liberal use of ornamental blind arcading. The apses do not project, but their internal position is marked by deep recesses in the wall.

Note the window (in itself a narrow slit), its large frame continued downward and upward. Below, it extends and unites with two ornamental plaques. Above, it is prolonged and crowned with an enormous cross. This is one of the favorite decorative schemes of Georgian architecture.

THE NATIONAL STYLE

MOSCOW

XVI Century

CHURCH OF THE ASCENSION

Kolomenskoye, near Moscow, 1532

PLATE XV

CHURCH OF THE ASCENSION

Kolomenskoye, near Moscow

Belfry and Water Tower dating from 15th and 17th century, respectively.

CHURCH OF THE ASCENSION

Kolomenskoye, near Moscow, 1532. Architect unknown.

Here, the characteristic features of the wood churches of Northern Russia were incorporated in masonry.

The church superstructure rests on an extensive base (Podklet) and is surrounded on three sides by covered galleries (Paperty) reached by covered strairways (Kryltza). Note, especially, the tent-shaped tower (shater), the receding tiers of ogee arches (Kokoshniki) leading up from the main superstructure to the octagonal base of the pyramidal tower. All those forms were, undoubtedly, borrowed from wood architecture.

The church is remarkable as a monument of a transition period. It demonstrates the highly individual approach of the Russian builder to forms and methods of masonry construction adopted from foreign masters. He uses them only as a means of recreating his traditional beloved wood church features "translating" them into masonry.

Courtesy Sovfoto, N.Y.

PLATE XVI

THE CATHEDRAL OF ST. BASIL THE BLESSED

(Vasiliy Blajennoi)

West Elevation.

Moscow, 1555–1560

Barma and Posnik, architects.

The Cathedral was built by Ivan IV (the Terrible) in commemoration of his conquest of the Tartar Khanate of Kazan. It represents in its exuberant architectural forms the triumph of the young Kingdom of Muscovy over its age long enemies and oppressors. Like its prototypes—the churches at Dyakovo, at Kolomenskoye and at Ostrovo—it embodies the characteristic features of the wood churches of North Russia, translating them into masonry.

It consists of a central dominant element (the Church of the Intercession) surrounded by eight churches and chapels (see plan), each one dedicated to a Saint whose feast day happened to coincide with the day of the eight decisive victories over the Tartars. These nine separate heterogeneous elements, connected only at the base, are highly individual in character. Yet they combine into a harmonious ensemble. Though decidedly non-conformist to academic canons of architectural aesthetics the rhythm of its component elements, the toy-like whimsicality of its details and the riot of colors create an effect of unforgettable exotic beauty and picturesqueness.

PLATE XVII

PLATE XVIII

GATEWAY TO THE CZAR'S ESTATE

Kolomenskoye, near Moscow. Second half of 17th century.

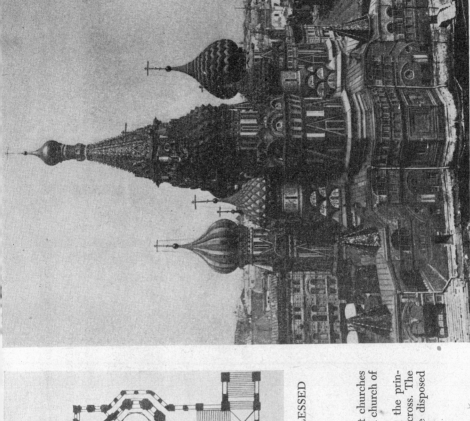

THE CATHEDRAL OF ST. BASIL THE BLESSED

Moscow, 1555–1560

Barma and Posnik, architects

General plan showing the disposition of the eight churches and chapels around the original core (the principal church of the Intercession of the Virgin).

The four secondary churches are arranged along the principal axes of the central church, thus forming a cross. The smaller chapels (which are lower in height) are disposed along the diagonal axes.

PLATE XIX   WEST ELEVATION

PLATE XX

FORTIFICATION WATCH TOWER

An example of the 17th century wood architecture of the North

PLATE XXI

THE NOVODEVICHI MONASTERY

Moscow, 16th and 17th century

General view

A highly picturesque assemblage of churches, chapels, watch-towers and belfries, some of them dating back to 1524. It was one of the several fortified monasteries in the chain of the outer defenses of the young capital.

Note the later additions of a decidedly non-military aspect: among them the great, many-storeyed Bell Tower (left background) built in 1688. Its general character and decorative features are strongly reminiscent of the then prevalent Moscow Baroque style.

THE CATHEDRAL OF OUR LADY OF SMOLENSK
East Elevation.

Moscow, 1524–1688

The Novodevichi Monastery.

PLATE XXIII

THE NOVODEVICHI MONASTERY

The Baroque of Moscow, 1688

The great Bell Tower of the Monastery. Note the storeyed tapering off arrangement of the tower, the balustrades, the highly ornamented window frames.

THE NARISHKIN BAROQUE
XVII Century

CHURCH OF THE HOLY VIRGIN
Village of Fili near Moscow, 1693
General scheme of the facade and plan.

One of the best examples of the so-called "Narishkin" or Moscow Baroque Period.

At the core of the general composition is the typical central part placed on an elevated terrace-like substructure (Podklet). This central part is surrounded on all sides by semi-circular elements, one of which serves as a sanctuary, the others as vestibules (Pritvori) or narthexes. An open gallery surrounds the four-lobed base. This gallery is served by three monumental stairways.

The general silhouette, pyramidal in form, and rising in several stages above the surrounding landscape is reminiscent of the stately composition of the Church of the Ascension at Kolomenskoye near Moscow.

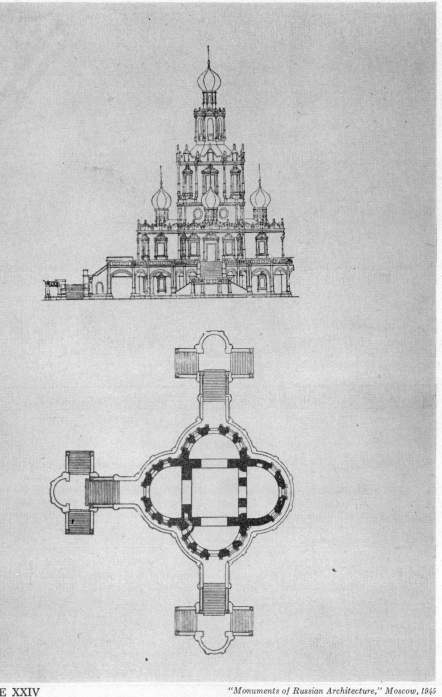

PLATE XXIV

"Monuments of Russian Architecture," Moscow, 1945

PLATE XXV

"Monuments of Russian Architecture," Moscow, 1945

CHURCH OF THE HOLY VIRGIN
Village of Fili near Moscow, 1693
West Elevation.

Drawing by V. E. Svinarsky.

The building is of brick and white stone. The large base which rises in three stages is surmounted by several octagonal prisms, diminishing in size and leading up to a small terminal cupola. The church bells are housed in the second octagon and thus the bell tower, formerly a separate structure, becomes an integral part of the church, giving the building a unified, more compact character. This combination church-bell-tower can be considered as a distinct architectural type among Russian churches, especially those erected by the great nobles on their country estates. It contributed to the creation of a universal type of structure and thus helped to eliminate local differences in church architecture. The evolution and spread of this feature coincided with the general tendency of further centralization of the growing 17th century Russian State.

PLATE XXVI   *"Monuments of Russian Architecture," Moscow, 1945*

CHURCH OF THE HOLY VIRGIN
Village of Fili near Moscow, 1693
Interior detail
Loge
North West Elevation.

The loge and its canopy, situated at the same level as the choir, is an important, richly decorated part of the interior. It was known as the "Tzar's place" where the Tzar or some great noble would have sat when he attended services there.

PLATE XXVII

"*Monuments of Russian Architecture,*" *Moscow, 1945*

CHURCH OF THE SAVIOUR
Village of Oubori, near Moscow, 1697
North West Elevation.

The elevated terrace (Podklet) is suppressed in height. The church therefore, lacks the imposing quality of its prototype at Fili, but the plan—though generally resembling the latter in outline—clearly indicates further development and enrichment of the four-lobed scheme, and shows a keener feeling for form.

PLATE XXVIII

CHURCH OF THE SAVIOUR
Village of Oubori, near Moscow, 1697
West Elevation.
I. G. Boukhvostov, Architect.
Measured drawing by V. Podkluchnikov.

One of the outstanding examples of the "Narishkin" or Moscow Baroque Period.

Note the gradual softening in outline, the progressive change in size and form of the openings—from the rectangular doors and windows of the first storey to the double-arched openings of the bell-tower.

The trimmings of the various architectural details are of white stone. The walls are of red brick.

"Monuments of Russian Architecture," Moscow, 1945

PLATE XXIX   CHURCH OF THE SAVIOUR
in the Village of Oubori, near Moscow, 1697

Exterior details. I. G. Boukhvostov, architect. Measured drawing by Podkluchnikov.

The exterior decorative scheme of this church, also of those at Fili and Troitzkoe-Likov, presents an unique amalgamation of Western European motifs with the basically traditional ornament of Russian architecture. Prominent in this scheme is a mutation of the classic order of the Renaissance—as conceived and interpreted by the Russian builders—combined with such whimsical elements of local architectural composition as parapets adorned with cockscombs, curiously curved pediments, carved finials and corbels and other details directly derived from the national forms of wood architecture.

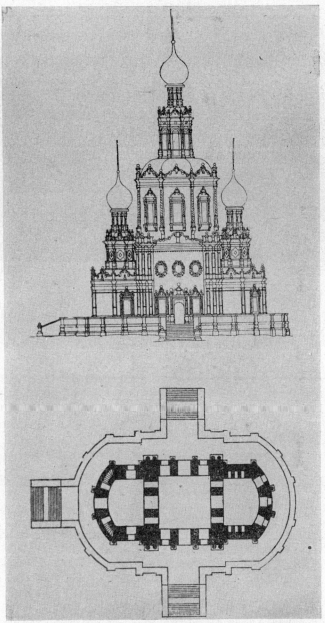

PLATE XXX *"Monuments of Russian Architecture," Moscow, 1945*

CHURCH OF THE HOLY TRINITY
in the Village of Troitzkoe-Likov near Moscow, about 1700

One of the examples of the so-called "Narishkin" or Moscow Baroque Period.

PLATE XXXI

"Monuments of Russian Architecture," Moscow, 1945

CHURCH OF THE HOLY TRINITY
in the Village of Troitzkoe-Likov, near Moscow, about 1700
Section.
Measured drawing by V. Podkluchnikov.

PLATE XXXII   *"Monuments of Russian Architecture," Moscow, 1945*

CHURCH OF THE HOLY TRINITY
in the Village of Troitzkoe-Likov, near Moscow, about 1700
North Elevation.
Measured drawing by V. Podkluchnikov.

The church is composed of three parts: a sanctuary, a place for the congregation and a vestibule (Pritvor). All three parts are placed on an elevated terrace and surrounded with a gallery reached by three wide stairways. The central part is a square structure surmounted by three tiers of octagons. The sanctuary and the vestibule are symmetrically rounded appurtenances, each one of which has its own small cupola.

PLATE XXXIII

CHURCH OF THE HOLY TRINITY
in the Village of Troitzkoe-Likov, near Moscow, about 1700
View of the Ikonostas.

The Ikonostas is the richly ornamented screen, separating the sanctuary from the nave of the church. It serves as a frame and a background for the many icons and pictures of saints given to the church by various donors. The central or the "Royal" door (Tzarskia vrata) is intended for the ceremonial entrance and exit of the priests only.

WOODEN ARCHITECTURE

PLATE XXXIV

CHURCH OF THE BOGORODITZA
(Mother of God)

Verkhovye, Province of Vologodsk, early 17th century

Cruciform in plan, built of logs. Note the slender tent-shaped towers on the roof gables and the main pyramidal tower with its octagonal drum, springing from the square center of the cruciform structure.

PLATE XXXV   *Photo by V. A. Plotnikov, Grabar*

THE OUSPENSKY CHURCH
Varzoug, Province of Archangel, 1674

(A good example of the Wood Architecture of the far North.)

Note the striking similarity between the wood church and the masonry Church of the Ascension at Kolomenskoye. The Varzoug church, though built nearly 150 years later, can be pointed out as the prototype for many of the masonry churches of the 16th century because it embodies some of the most characteristic features of the wood architecture of the North that were "translated" so happily into masonry.

THE 22 DOME CHURCH OF THE TRANSFIGURATION
at the Kizhi Cemetery (Pogost), Kizhi, Province of Olonetsk, 1714

In plan it follows the traditional form of the tent-church: an octa-gon—to which, on each alternate side—were added square projec-tions, thus converting it into a cross. Instead of crowning it with the usual tent, the builder chose to break away from tradition, and superimposed octagon upon octagon in a series of steps, crowning each step with a "bochka" and bulbous dome thus achieving the unusual effect of 22 domes. What's more, the builder, in doing this, actually defied the existing canonical regulations which limited the number of cupolas to nine. (Symbolic of the nine grades of angels or saints.) He rose above the narrow traditions of the time and thus created something highly individual.

The result of this extraordinary combination—of simple and com-plex elements, traditional and revolutionary forms and methods—is the creation of an extremely picturesque fairy-like structure ex-pressing the unique genius of the Russian builders of the North.

PLATE XXXVI

Courtesy Sovfoto, N.Y.

PLATE XXXVII   CHURCH OF THE INTERCESSION

Kizhi, on Lake Onega (the far North), early 18th century

Detail, showing the upper octagonal portion of the structure, supporting the central dome (cupola), surrounded by eight smaller ones in a circle.

PLATE XXXVIII

Photo by V. A. Plotnikov—Grabar

A DESERTED WOODEN BELFRY
in the Province of Olonetzk, Danilov Hermitage

(18th Century Architecture of the far North)

A small and nostalgic example of a "tented" eight-sided wooden bell tower in the Old Believers (Raskolniki) Hermitage of Danilov, closed by an edict of Catherine the Great.

ST. PETERSBURG
XVIII and XIX Centuries

PLATE XXXIX

MONUMENT TO PETER I
St. Petersburg, 1766–1782
Falconet, Sculptor

THE PLAN OF ST. PETERSBURG

Project, 1717. Leblond, architect.

The plan as "idealized" by Leblond never became a reality. He evidently did not quite grasp the magnitude of the problem, nor fully evaluate its topographical elements.

THE SMOLNEY CONVENT (MODEL)

St. Petersburg, 1748-1765. Count F. B. Rastrelli, architect.

From the Collection of the Academy of Arts.

The beautifully carved and colored model is minutely worked out to the very last architectural and decorative detail. It shows that Rastrelli—one of the great proponents of the Baroque—had conceived a grandiose, compact architectural ensemble, every element of which was studied out very carefully in its interrelation to the whole. The profusion, variety and richness of the Baroque architectural and decorative detail is overwhelming. The color effects— the heavily gilt ornament against a background of turquoise walls, white columns, cornices and light silvery roofs—make an unforgettable impression. In the words of Matveev (the author of a Monograph on Rastrelli), it was all calculated to impress the beholder with the splendor and sumptuousness of the ensemble. It was to demonstrate to the "people" the piety of the "Little Mother Queen" (Elizabeth) and her great generosity in the beautification of the "House-of-God."

PLATE XL

PLATE XLI   THE ENSEMBLE OF THE SMOLNEY CONVENT

Leningrad (St. Petersburg), 1748–1835.

F. B. Rastrelli, architect.

The Cathedral was conceived as the central and principal element of the ensemble. The huge bell-tower (shown on the model), 465 feet in height, was envisioned as the main entrance motif but was never built.

PLATE XLII

"Leningrad," Iskoustvo, 1943

THE PETROPAVLOVSKY CATHEDRAL
Leningrad (St. Petersburg), 1714–1733.
D. Trezzini, architect.

PLATE XLIII   THE PETERHOFF PALACE
Near St. Petersburg, 1722–1750. B. Rastrelli, architect.

Central part of Facade. View from the main Cascade.

The Palace was originally built by Leblond in 1722. Some 20 years later, Queen
Elizabeth, whose tastes ran to gayety and pleasure, commissioned Rastrelli (her
favorite architect) to remodel certain parts of it in a richer more flamboyant style.

PLATE XLIV

THE CHATEAU AT GATCHINA

Near St. Petersburg, 1766–1777. Rinaldi, architect.

The building quite austere and forbidding in character is somewhat reminiscent of the Spanish Escorial of F¹·lippe II. The interior is in the style of Louis XVI. The park contains a number of Pavilions and "Temples" in the French manner

PLATE XLV

THE GRAND PALACE AT TZARSKOE SELO

Detail of wing

PLATE XLVI

THE GRAND PALACE AT TZARSKOE SELO

The Elizabethan Rococo Period, 1749–1756. Bartolomeo Rastrelli, architect.

A very large (about 1000 ft. long) and sumptuous palace, richly decorated with sculpture and ornament, in an impressive setting—a symbol of the wealth and splendour of Queen Elizabeth. Its interior, containing the celebrated Chinese and Amber Salons; the Grand Gallery and Picture Gallery is considered to be one of the best examples of the Russian Rococo.

PLATE XLVII

THE PAVLOVSK PALACE

Pavlovsk, near St. Petersburg, 1782–1785

Built for the Tzarevitch Paul (Pavel). Cameron, architect.

Designed in the grand manner of the Italian Villa, it is decorated with columns and crowned with a flat dome, reminiscent of the Roman Pantheon. The building contains some magnificently decorated rooms, (the Italian Room under the dome, the Greek Room, and others) and it houses a wonderful collection of Louis XVI furniture. The garden is in the English manner, and is known as one of the best specimens of the late 18th century. The surrounding park is filled with many lovely Pavilions, "Temples," and Statuary.

PLATE XLVIII

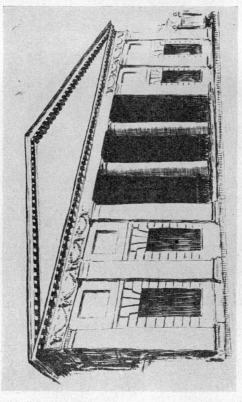

THE STATE BANK
St. Petersburg. G. Quarenghi, architect.
Detail of wing. Note the use of simple Doric columns and pilasters.

THE STATE BANK
St. Petersburg. G. Quarenghi, architect.
General schematic plan.

PLATE XLIX

THE STATE BANK

St. Petersburg, circa 1790. Giacomo Quarenghi, architect.

Side elevation. One of the many many works of this gifted architect, the last of the Great Catherine architectural epoch, and the precursor of the Alexandrian Classic Period (The "Empire" Style). His works show a definite break with the art of the Rastrelli Baroque. His architecture is relatively severe and simple. Its grandeur and beauty is achieved mainly by the exquisite refinement of general proportions, line and detail.

PLATE L

THE SENATE BUILDING

St. Petersburg, 1829–1835. Carlo Rossi, architect.

Detail, showing treatment at corner. Note the double column projection motif at each corner.

PLATE LI

THE ARCH OF TRIUMPH

LINKING THE SENATE AND SYNOD BUILDINGS

St. Petersburg, 1829–1835. Carlo Rossi, architect.

The architect, who usually exercised great restraint in the use of decoration has, this time, chosen to make use of an abundance of architectural and sculptural forms, bordering upon the Baroque, with the result that the arch has a somewhat ostentatious and pompous air.

PLATE LII

THE KAZAN CATHEDRAL

St. Petersburg, 1801–1811. A. N. Voronikhin, architect.

In its general conception, the Cathedral—in the form of a Latin cross, with its dome and Colonnade—is somewhat reminiscent of the Roman Pantheon and the Basilica of St. Peter.

Though unfinished (as the architect's plans called for a second colonnade) the Cathedral—because of the magnificence of its interior, the elegance of its dome silhouette, and the lovely diaphanous quality of its colonnade—is one of the outstanding examples of the Alexandrian Classic Period.

"Leningrad," Iskoustvo, 1943

THE KAZAN CATHEDRAL. DETAIL OF GRILLE.
Leningrad (St. Petersburg), 1801–1811. A. Voronikhin, architect.

THE ADMIRALTY

St. Petersburg, 1806–1810. A. D. Zakharov, architect.

Main Facade. The building, monumental and military in character, occupies an entire block. The main facade, about 1400 ft. long, is composed of three colonnaded elements. The central element, the cube-like tower-portal is richly decorated and it serves as a pedestal for a smaller colonnaded cube which, in turn, supports a very tall slender spire, the famous "Admiralty Needle."

PLATE LIV

THE ADMIRALTY

St. Petersburg, 1806–1810. A. D. Zakharov, architect.

Detail of the Main Portal. Its large surfaces are treated very sensitively with ornament and high-relief sculpture. The statuary groups and the sculptured frieze, symbolizing the birth of the Russian navy are by Schedrin.

PLATE LV

"Leningrad," Iskoustvo, 1943

THE ADMIRALTY TOWER
Leningrad (St. Petersburg), 1806–1815. A. Zakharov, architect.

PLATE LVI

THE ADMIRALTY

One of the *pavilions*, facing the river Neva.

PLATE LVII

"Leningrad," Iskoustvo, 1943

THE ADMIRALTY ENTRANCE GATE
Leningrad (St. Petersburg), 1806–1815. A. Zakharov, architect.

PLATE LVIII   *Courtesy Sovfoto, N.Y.*

THE CATHEDRAL OF SAINT ISAAC
Leningrad, (St. Petersburg), 1819–1858. Richard de Montferrand, architect.

This enormous Cathedral with its golden dome dominates the skyline of the city. It is somewhat reminiscent of St. Pauls in London, but surpasses it in the breathtaking scale of its columns, the beauty and sumptuousness of its marbles and mosaics and ornamental detail.

The architect won his commission in open competition with native and foreign architects.

MOSCOW
XVIII and XIX Centuries

THE MOSCOW RIVER EMBANKMENT ALONG THE SOUTHEAST KREMLIN WALL

The Vodozvodnaïa Tower is in foreground to the left.

PLATE LIX

THE CHURCH OF THE TRINITY

Ostankino, near Moscow, 1668

An example of the last phase of the Moscow Baroque style. Note the bulbous cupolas perched on the highly attenuated drums supported, in their turn, on two tiers of ogee "kokoshniki." The window frames are very ornate and the brick work is complex and florid. To the right is the 18th century villa of the Sheremetyev family.

PLATE LX   THE OLD LENIN PUBLIC LIBRARY (THE HOUSE OF PASHKOV)

Moscow, 1784. V. I. Bajenov, Architect.

It was originally designed as a town house for the wealthy Pashkov family. Outwardly, it still retains the character-istic features of the great "City-Estate" manors prevalent in and about Moscow in the 18th century. Later on it was remodeled to house the collections of the Roumyantzev Museum, and at present it is the "Old" Lenin Public Library.

PLATE LXI

THE MOSCOW STATE UNIVERSITY

M. Kasakov, architect

The building gutted during the fire of 1812 was rebuilt by D. Giliardi in 1817.

PLATE LXII

HOUSE NEAR THE TVERSKAYA GATE
Moscow, circa 1825. Beavais, architect.

PLATE LXIII

A GARDEN "TEMPLE." THE NAIDEYNOV MANOR
Moscow, circa 1830. Dementyi I. Gilardi, architect.

This "Temple" is one of the many charming elements of the Naideynov family "City-Estate" situated on the banks of the Yauza River in Moscow proper.

The designer of this Manor, D. Gilardi is one of the last of the great family of "Italian-Russian" architects, whose individual and national genius was transformed during their long residence in Russia and thoroughly assimilated into the creative stream of their adopted country.

PLATE LXIV

THE GOLOVIN HOUSE
Moscow, 1830

Entrance Detail

PLATE LXV   THE LENIN MUSEUM (FORMERLY THE MOSCOW DOUMA)
Late 19th century. D. Chichagov, architect.

This is a fairly representative example of the Pseudo-Russian style of the eighties, a product of, the then, prevalent infatuation with the revival and reinterpretation of the 17th Century Moscow architecture.

PLATE LXVI

THE HISTORICAL MUSEUM

Red Square, Moscow, 1883. V. O. Sherwood, architect.

Another example of the Pseudo-Russian style as interpreted by V. O. Sherwood (an Englishman). For his models he took the Cathedral of St. Basil (located at the opposite end of the Red Square), the wood palace at Kolomenskoye, and the brick churches of Iaroslavl. He did not miss anything of this so-called "Genuine-Russian" detail and

PLATE LXVII
A MOSCOW BACK-YARD
from the Painting by V. D. Polenov, 1874

A bit of Moscow of the Seventies as the artist perceived it, conveying the mood
of the Russian provincial hinterland transfered to the heart of Moscow.

PLATE LXVIII

THE BOLSHOI THEATRE

Sverdlov Square, Moscow, 1824. O. I. Beauvais, architect.

The theatre is one of the great landmarks of 19th century Moscow. In the foreground is the entrance to the Okhotny Ryad Subway Station.

PLATE LXIX

THE PRESIDIUM BUILDING

The U.S.S.R. Academy of Sciences, Moscow

Part II

THE REVOLUTIONARY
AND CONTEMPORARY SOVIET
ARCHITECTURE

THE PALACE OF THE SOVIETS, MOSCOW
North West view. Photo from model (as of 1937).

Professor V. G. Helfreich, Academicians B. M. Iofan and V. A. Schouko, architects.

The Revolutionary Period

THE GREATEST UPHEAVAL in the history of Russian art was caused by the Revolution of 1917. It liberated forces in that enormous country, the existence of which nobody suspected. The Revolution, though at first directed against Absolutism and intolerable social conditions, destroyed in its path all the other hitherto accepted tenets in politics, economics, religion and art. Its aim had been to erect upon the ruins of a destroyed civilization a new civilization based upon entirely new principles, directed by new incentives and governed by new laws.

It is well to bear in mind that in Russia most of her cultural efforts had been identified with a spirit of violent protest and struggle, a struggle that, though changing its objectives, had been going on for centuries; first against the Tartar invasion and its attempted imposition of an alien culture upon Russia, then against the early Romanovs, who tried to impose a European civilization upon a people still in the patriarchal stage of development. Later on the revolt was against the unbearable social conditions, remnants of feudalism and the relics of an Asiatic barbarism. With the advance of the modern industrial era and the awakening of the Russian middle classes, an infiltration from Europe of an irrational Classicism and a sugary romanticism could be noted. To combat that there sprang up the Russian National School which set itself against the cosmopolitan eclectic estheticism of the upper classes. It was this movement that sired the revival of Russian antiquity, only again to be counteracted by the strong European "New Art" movement, and all the other currents in the art esthetic that paraded in Russia under the name of "Art Nouveau," "Art Moderne," Viennese Secession," "Decadence," etc.

DEMAGOGY AND THE CHAOS IN THE ARCHITECTURAL ESTHETIC

The architectural esthetic, no less than that of the other arts, was affected by the general spirit of restlessness and discontent, by the ominous storm of revolution that was brewing in the country. It was in a state of confusion, constantly swayed by theoretic polemics between the older and the younger schools of the profession. It was only natural that the younger architects were fired by the new radical ideas prevailing at that time in Western Europe. Anything that was revolutionary, anything that claimed a break with the past was, ipso facto, better than the old and so Constructivism, Functionalism, Utilitarianism, and many other Isms became the things a la mode, even de rigeur. On the other hand anything that smacked of the retrospective, of Slavophilism, of the emotional or the lyrical was derided and declared reactionary.

These verbal battles had been going on for a number of years. Anyone familiar with the Russian passion for discussion, dissection and analysis of ideas can easily imagine the interminable hours of debate, the acreage of printed pages consumed in citing, quoting and interpreting the maxims of Marx, Engels, Lenin, Stalin, which might shed in any way, however remote, the true light upon their own pet conceptions of some Isms, and thereby point the way towards the "only truth," to the salvation of architecture and the other arts from the taint of "decadent capitalism."

The effect of the first few years of the revolution upon the art esthetic of those days could be characterized as an incentive to rebellion against accepted theories, established routines and especially against opportunism in art. The spirit of unrest and suppressed fury that filled the very air in those days had brought about a breakaway from the domination of the academicians, the older architects, the pedants who had ceased to create, but who had the aura of learning about them, the authority of experience and the backing of the formerly vested and entrenched interests. In a word it was a rebellion of the young against the old, the beginners against the already arrived and successful. Having seized control, the "Left" artistic and architectural fraternity of Russia embarked upon a period of feverish and intensive quest. In this group there were representatives of all the new schools, of all possible shades and tendencies. There were the Realists and the Impressionists, but most of all there were the Futurists, the Cubists and the Suprematists. It is not hard to explain this seeming paradox, since they all belonged to the revolutionary "Left" in art. Though, in principle, absolutely alien to Communism they were given free play because of their professed "Left" tendencies.

Futurism in its various shades, so far as it stood for breaking up traditional patterns and old rhythms, for inciting and hypnotizing the masses; so long as it preached vehement action, absolute individualism in ethics and anarchism in government was welcome to pre-Bolshevistic revolutionary Russia. Any doctrine that denied the accepted formulas, anything that proclaimed the spirit of revolt was welcomed, as long as it was against tradition, against regimentation.

BOLSHEVISM VS. ANARCHY AS AN ARCHITECTURAL PHILOSOPHY

The second period can be characterized as the reaction to the spirit of anarchy and individualism in art, which in its social implications threatened to become a serious menace to the Bolshevist doctrine of strict party unity and discipline in government. The reign of the Futurists and the Cubists was cut short. As early as 1919 Kamenev, the President of the Moscow Soviet, declared in a speech: "Enough of this clownish performance. The workers' government must decisively stop the support which it has given to all kinds of Futurists, Cubists, and Imagists—all these contortionists—they are not proletarian artists and their art is not ours. They are the product of Bourgeois corruption, Bourgeois degeneration." As a result of that, and many other utterances of the same nature by other Bolshevik officials, there began a campaign against "Bourgeois" art; the dominance of Futurism and Cubism was undermined, and they were declared enemies of "proletarian" art.

A new movement toward proletarian art and culture was initiated by the Proletcult group, a name derived from the two words "Proletarian Culture" telescoped together. It advocated a revaluation of the old cultural and artistic heritage, and the building up of a new culture. It rejected individualism which is the vital principle in "Bourgeois" culture, substituting for it the proletarian principle of Collectivism in culture and art. This movement did influence many of the younger writers, artists, and architects, but in the sober atmosphere of Soviet Rationalism and Materialism it was destined to fade away. The Bolshevik leaders realized soon enough that culture and art, no matter what you may label them, cannot be manufactured or created to order. In a speech delivered in 1920, Lenin said: "It is impossible for us to solve the question of proletarian culture without a clear understanding and exact knowledge of that culture which was created in the course of humanity's development; it is only by remaking this that proletarian culture is possible. . . ." Three years later, Lenin wrote: "While we are chattering about proletarian culture and its relation to Bourgeois culture, the situation is none too good . . . Our progress in comparison with Czarist times (1897) is much too slow . . . This shows how much hard work there is still to be done in order to attain the level of an ordinary civilized nation in Western Europe. . . ." [1]

CONSTRUCTIVISM IN ARCHITECTURE

Other Bolshevik leaders have also denied the possibilities of a pure proletarian culture, though some of them maintained that the transition period would produce a "Transition Art," an art distinctively new under the influence of the Revolution. One phase in the esthetics of that "Transition Art" was destined to influence the direction of Russian architecture and the applied arts in a very marked way. This was Constructivism. The essence of its teachings was somewhat akin to that of the Bauhaus School in Dessau, Germany. Its principal exponents were such talented artists and architects as Tatlin, Lissitzky, and Professor Ladovsky.

In a practical way the most significant aspect of Construc-

[1] Collected Works of Nikolai Lenin, Vol XXV, p. 387; Vol. XXVII, p. 387.

tivism was contained, not so much in its "new" esthetic theories as, in the principle of Utilitarianism, which that school stressed. Architecture, they maintained, must be stripped of everything that is not rational, not appropriate, and not useful. Every element, every detail of the structure must earn its existence only when it is perfectly useful and economical, only when it has the feeling of a "material awareness," and only when the elements making up the structure can be manufactured on a quantity production basis by machinery.

The leaders of this school maintained that the Revolution must reflect itself in an art and an architecture rooted in the current production processes of the land's industry and agriculture. Architecture, according to them, must become a new art which would express the collective aims of the masses. By preaching its sermon through mass, form and color to consciousness it should educate and inspire the people to bigger and greater achievements in social progress. This, they said, could be accomplished by a suitable choice of materials which are the products of the Soviet industry: steel, concrete, glass, wood; by the architect's abandoning his aloof position of the dilletante and theoretical snob, and making a thorough first hand craftsman's study of the various materials, combining them with precision into forms that would express the desired objectives. Through skillful and successful use of the distinct properties and characteristic virtues of those materials the new architect would endow his work with the quality of constructiveness and organization in the life about him. And so, the architect must become engineer and workman first. The artistic urge or the artistic stir in the designer must express itself in the organic beauty, in the organic decorative quality of the structure, in the mass and in the form-revealing lines of its various elements.

Among the practical applications of Constructivism to architectural design were the much heralded projects of Tatlin's "Monument to the Third International" and Lissitsky's project for a speaker's rostrum. Both of them were to embody the latest mechanical and constructional achievements, they were to synthesize the creative impulses of art and the utilitarian achievements of science. Neither of these projects were ever realized. The infatuation for Constructivism began to wane. The wide discrepancy between its alleged utilitarianism and its unbridled flights of fantasy was too marked. Its opponents were not slow to stress that and to ridicule the entire movement mercilessly. The older more practical schools and groupings were becoming more assertive, and the influence of contemporary work in Germany, Sweden and Holland was becoming more noticeable. New tendencies were being multiplied while the still older ones were being re-interpreted. Disputes and clashes of opinion were growing. Dominating them all were the practical considerations of getting to work and the pressing need to build up the ruins inherited from the civil war. The liberal principle of "laissez faire, laissez passer" could no longer be graciously tolerated, and so the Soviet Union embarked upon the third period, the period of less talk and more practical work.

THE ARCHITECTS OF THE OLD SCHOOL

The Russian architect who had matured during the period of disintegration of the Czarist regime was a dreamer, a romantic, an esthete at heart, very seldom a revolutionist, practically never a Marxist. His Parnassian attitude had to give way to the revolutionary idea of architecture as conceived by the younger generation: architecture as an integral part of the life of the masses. It was a bitter pill, indeed, for him to swallow his professional pride and intellectual aloofness and to be made to accept what he considered a lot of twaddle of the proponents of the Marx-Engels social theories as affecting the architectural esthetic. However (quoting Mr. Lozowick freely), the inexorable "law of social gravitation to the ruling class had gradually become operative,"[1] so that members of practically every shade and tendency, sooner or later had to switch over, at least outwardly, toward the prevailing social-order philosophy and its interpretation of the art esthetic.

Many of the able, established architects carried over their professional activities into the new era. Among them were the academicians Shchoussev (designer of the Lenin Mausoleum), Schouko and Joltovsky (one of the winners of the first prize in the Palace of the Soviets Competition). The historians of Russian architecture, Igor Grabar, and Professor N. Brunov kept up their brilliant work. Some of the die-hards left the country. Those who remained, at first, refused to compromise with what they called "hooliganism" and illiteracy in the arts. They abhorred the young lusty prophets of the revolution and the new principles enunciated by them, and therefore chose to remain either inactive, refusing to cooperate with the young leaders, or maintained a state of scoffing neutrality or downright hostility.

The fate of the Russian architect of the old school was not a very happy one, especially in the first few years of the Revolution. The social classes, to whom he had catered professionally, had been dethroned. Like most of his brethren in the professional field he was rudely shaken out of his comfortable berth, torn from a position of respect and security, and forced

[1] L. Lozowick, "Voices of October." The Vanguard Press, New York.

by material want and hunger to sell his intellectual integrity and professional attainments to a regime which he disliked and which he considered and hoped to be only a short-lived one. The other alternative was to leave the country by devious ways, swell the already large numbers of unemployed Russian emigré professionals in Berlin, Paris, Prague, etc., and from there enviously watch the dizzying "tempo" of construction in Russia.

THE PRECURSORS OF THE NEW ESTHETIC

On the other hand, the young ardent and aggressive radicals in the architectural and the other professional ranks were quick to take advantage of the marvelous opportunity presented to them. They did not lose any time in placing themselves in key positions for directing and guiding the new artistic and professional policies, and proclaiming the new evangel of a socialized architecture. It did not take long to formulate and promulgate the cardinal maxims: that architecture like all art is a class art, that it must reflect the new social system, that the collapse of the old social order should also mean the collapse of the old architectural esthetic which "capitalism" had sired and fostered. Just as the old religious fervor and aspirations of Medievalism had created the great cathedrals, in a style expressive of the ideals of that time; just as the Renaissance, following the disintegration of Medievalism, had created a style perfectly suited to the new individualism of that epoch, so must, the radicals said, Collectivism and Communism, superseding dying Capitalism, create a new expression of the esthetic, a new style suitable to the needs and psychology of the new collectivity; a style that would reflect the democratic ideals of the new-born state.

DEMOCRATIZATION OF ARCHITECTURE

The revision of the architectural esthetic had to be along the lines of the Marx-Engels concepts of art. Art had to be democratized, it had to be brought to the people. No longer should architecture serve the pampered nobility, the aristocratic idlers and the wealthy, but it should serve the masses. Instead of building cathedrals and churches, instead of building private palaces and villas, in synthetic styles, or insipidly imitating the pre-Peter architectural epoch, let us, the communist said, build palaces for the Soviets; let us build theaters and museums that will serve the masses, provide decent housing, schools, libraries, club houses, hospitals, and stadiums for the people. Instead of moping over warmed-over ornamental modes, "facades" and senile stylistic systems of the past, let us draw our inspiration from our own times, from the new morality around us. Let us build of such materials as we have at hand, and in such a manner as to make the best use of their inherent qualities. Let our buildings be the living expression of the longings and aspirations of the masses, of the new faith and the new social ideal.

In accordance with this new philosophy, new esthetic canons were advanced. Purely "artistic" preoccupations were scorned. The word "art" became anathema, something to shun. "Art for art's sake" was something to avoid, something to wage war upon. The new credo taught that the architect's function is not to decorate life but to help to organize it. His duty is to help to mold the new social personality. He should devote his creative abilities to the productive industrial processes and so "re-build and re-fashion the environment that it may function with mechanical precision."

The new creed, the new philosophy in architecture, was

essentially materialistic, perfectly sufficient unto itself, blindly believing in its rightness to the point of being belligerent. It disdained fancy and pretended to be bored by idealism as conceived in the "Bourgeois" meaning of the word. It was born of a fanatical desire to break completely with the past, with anything even remotely connected, or slightly tainted with "Bourgeois" civilization. It rudely interrupted the various decadent and eclectic movements prevailing in the Russia of the pre-war period and imposed upon the endeavor of all arts a unity of attitude, and a similarity of theme. In the words of Professor Sidorov, "Art as a special form of ideology must be switched into the general circuit of Soviet ideology." [1] Works of architecture should make an effort to state one aspect or another of the Marxist dogma, to use fairly standardized devices in order to preach the new faith and hope.

THE BASES FOR THE NEW ESTHETIC

Contemporary Soviet architecture bases itself, first of all, on the essential Marxian principle that "architectural art is a dialectic unity of technic and ideology." It does not contain any Nihilism, and it does not deny itself the demands of formal expression. It orientates itself primarily on the "functional" peculiarities of the given problem and every one of its elements but it does not forget its ideologically-formal requirements. To quote Professor Brunov freely: "the Marxian advances the concept of an integrated architectural whole in which technically-functional and ideologically-formal moments are brought to a unity." [2]

Functionalism, in so far as it stood in opposition to eclec-

[1] Professor A. Sidorov, "VOKS," 1931. No. 10–12. Moscow.
[2] N. Brunov. VOKS No. 10–12, 1931, Moscow.

ticism, to lack of principles, to extreme formalistic schools of thought, had been indeed very persuasive. Up to nearly 1930, it had been one of the guiding articles of faith, and it had played a very important and necessary part in the work of the young Soviet architects. But extreme, so-called post-Functionalism, which denies that architecture is an art and which transforms a building into a machine, is frowned upon. On the other hand, extreme Formalism, which considers architecture as an abstract form, as something "isolated from life" and subject only to the "eternal" laws of beauty, does not fare any better.

The two most important argumentative points, around which revolves the discussion of the type of architecture suitable for a Communist culture, are: first, the relation of man to machine; second, the relation of the civilization and culture of a Communist society to the past. Both of these are indicative of the ideological and artistic tenor of Soviet esthetics. Constructivism and Symbolism, which influenced the work of the early post-Revolutionary Russian architects were dismissed as merely infantile and unrelated to life. Extreme, stark Functionalism is attacked because it stresses excessively the consideration of technique and because, in its extreme devotion to technical processes, it has become identified with the enslavement of man to machine. Extreme Fuctionalism is unsuitable for Soviet architecture because, it is argued, it is the materialization and expression of the ideals of Capitalism, a "system that is subjecting great masses of humanity to technical developments, while there is an epoch beginning in the USSR that is going to be characterized by the subjugation of technical developments to man." [1]

[1] Freely quoted from the Official Report of N. P. Zapletin, Secretary of the Commission of Experts for the Palace of the Soviets' Competition.

The second point is the relation of present culture to that of the past. Again, it is pointed out that Lenin recognized the fact that a revolutionary society was the cultural as well as the practical, heir to past accumulated wealth, that the past must not be rejected in toto but re-appraised and re-worked. Instead of scornfully dismissing the "Bourgeois" past, one must first master its artistic and engineering achievements and only then endeavor to transcend them.

The express aim of Soviet architecture is to master all the technical achievements of Western Europe and America in order to be able to inaugurate the construction of the new social types. In this intention can be found the essential similarities and differences between the advanced architecture of Western Europe and America and that of the Soviet Union. The similarity lies in striving for the technique of and the know-how for the realization of a project. It expresses itself in those formative elements, developed in the light of modern technically-productive processes. The differences consist in a demand for ideological contents in architecture, in its conscious concurrence with the tasks of social construction. These differences are apparent in those formative elements which spring from the basis of the new social order, the new social needs and problems, the new production modes and habits, and all the new conditions of existence which differentiate the U.S.S.R. from the rest of the world.

A brief outline of the theoretical platforms of the important architectural societies that were active in the U.S.S.R. may give us an idea of the main currents in Soviet architecture, that were particularly noticeable in the twenties and the early thirties. It may give a clue to a few of the riddles that have baffled the foreign observers for the last twenty-five years.

THE RUSSIAN ARCHITECTURAL ASSOCIATIONS

There were several architectural associations (groupings) in Russia identified by their various platforms. Their theory of the architectural esthetic and their works were motivated by what they claimed to be, distinct ideological and methodological concepts. These differences, though somewhat tenuous and inconsequential to the American architect, seemed nevertheless vital to the Russians, judging by the lengthy and vigorous discussions in the press devoted to these various principles and the not-too-friendly polemics between these groups. Though outwardly differing in their concepts of the architectural esthetic they were all trying to adapt architecture to the new circumstances.

Chief among them was the SASS (formerly the OSA) the Architectural Sector of Socialist Construction, organized in 1925. The members of this group were the proponents of Functionalism, claiming that this method is based on the theory of Dialectic materialism. Architecture to them was primarily a science. They stressed the engineering function in architecture and the "use" reason for every detail that goes into the design of their buildings. They were against architectural forms for the purpose of "embracing the whole sphere of feeling and the whole complicated complex of human emotions and thoughts." They waged merciless war on eclecticism, on "style" in building, on Formalism and on Revivalism, as something that is a remnant of the hostile capitalist ideology. To them an architectural creation must be the result of a thorough study of the living social and productive processes, and of the "technology" and static qualities of the structural materials. Among some of the better known men of this group were M. Ginsburg, the designer of many important buildings in all parts of the Union—the three ubiquitous Vesnin brothers,—the famous but much berated Leonidov and Kuznetzov.

The ASNOVA group, (Association of New Architects) organized in 1923, was somewhat more moderate, somewhat formalistic. They, too, were against Eclecticism and they stressed "esthetic rationalism" in architecture, defining the latter as "the economy of psychic energy in the comprehension of the spatial and functional characteristics of a structure" (Professor Ladovsky). The members of this group were not opposed to foreign ideas and they made propaganda for Le Corbusier and the "Bauhaus." They were, as one of the leaders declared, "for an everlasting objective beauty of forms in architecture expressing the power and the weakness, the greatness and the pettiness, the finite and the infinite." In general the ASNOVA based its ideology and its method on an idealistic interpretation of philosophy and on a formalistic esthetic. Among the better known proponents of this school were the architects, Ladovsky, Krinsky, Dokuchaev, Bunin, and Turkus.

The VOPRA group (The Society of the All-Union Proletarian Architects), was founded in 1929. The members of this group championed a class, a proletarian architecture, but, paradoxically enough, stressed the role of *art* in architecture. They were against Constructivism which according to them had brought about the negation of art, substituting for the latter technique and engineering. One of the principal planks in its platform was "the expressing through architecture the deepest thoughts, strivings, and ideals of the working class." They were against Formalism which according to them is something foreign to the social utilitarian problems, something that smacks of Utopia and baseless fantasy, a "theory which arrives at abstract architectural forms through laboratory methods, forcing into those pre-accepted forms the contents of the building." Prominent members of this group were: Alabyan, Babourov, Zaslavsky, and Vlasov.

As the reader will notice, these cleavages in the interpretation of the architectural esthetic were not of terrific import. They all claimed a kinship of their theories with the Marx-Engels concepts of art and architecture. Perhaps the real distinction was the fact that the first group was composed of the more active practicing architects; the leaders of the second group belonged to the academic branch of the profession, while the members of the third group claimed the virtue of being more orthodox in their "party" leanings. This group (VOPRA) had assumed the role of a stabilizer, as it were, curbing extreme post-Functionalism on one hand, and the groundless Utopia of Formalism on the other hand.

In 1930, those of the architectural groups, with definite leanings toward the Soviet ideological platform, banded together into an all-union architectural scientific society (VANO), maintaining, however, their separate "sectarian" aesthetic concepts of architecture.

In April 1932 an official government decree was issued, directing the reorganization of the entire structure of the existing artistic and literary societies.

In compliance with that directive, all the various functioning architectural, theatrical, musical and literary societies were to be liquidated; their various "sectarian" cells dissolved, and each professional group reorganized into a central federation, where they would continue to work and collaborate, contributing their individual and collective efforts towards, the enrichment of Soviet culture.

A few months later, the Federation of Soviet Architects was

formed, (The SSA) uniting the various groups: the conservatives, the centrists and the radicals.[1]

The SSA is the official guiding body for the Soviet architects. In it are centralized the educational, professional and social activities of its members. It functions as the central exchange of ideas, as interpreter and clarifier of the accepted ideological platform. It acts as guide and teacher for the younger members and assists in the professional and artistic development of the more mature membership. It integrates the activities of the various experts working in the building field and is the arbiter of all disputable points. It makes all important decisions, organizes competitions and makes all principal nominations.

The local "sectors" or branches of the SSA conduct for its members clubs (The "Houses of the Architect") libraries, restaurants and organize all sorts of educational, sport and recreational activities.

Through its local clubs the SSA conducts local and regional forums and group visits from one region to another. It arranges for interprofessional meetings with the federations of other professions and arts for an interchange of ideas and discussions of the common cultural problems.

Following one of the basic Soviet tenets of collective work, the member architects must submit their work for collective criticism by their fellow co-workers, experts in the related fields; workers in the various building trades and the future tenants. No project is approved by the authorities without proof of it having been submitted by the designer to public criticism.

The Soviet architects are working under terrific pressure,

[1] Among the directors of the governing body are some of the best known, leading Soviet architects: V. A. Vesnin, chairman. K. C. Alabyan, vice chairman. D. E. Arkin, secretary. The official organ of the SSA is the "ARCHITECTURA U.S.S.R." a monthly review. K. C. Alabyan, Editor-in-chief.

as though a war time spirit still ruled. They are straining every nerve, but very often are able to supply no more than mere sketches or diagrams of what is to be built, and perhaps built many times over, in different parts of the Union. In the earlier stages of reconstruction architectural inspection ·by the designer was almost impossible because of long distances and lack of time. It is not surprising that things were badly done, but that they were done at all, when one considers that the Russian architect had to contend with a constant shortage of skilled craftsmen, shortage of materials, lack of well seasoned timber and hardwoods and a severe climate, where anywhere from four to six months of heavy snows and rain prevail. On the other hand, some of the handicaps, that the American architect is hampered by, are unknown to the Russians. Since the land is nationalized—eccentric and freakish lot-lines practically do not exist. The private entrepreneur and the building contractor have been supplanted by government building trusts. Speculative building projects, manipulation of real estate values or building rental considerations are unknown. The Russian, therefore, enjoys unmatched opportunities in the free development of functional planning. Judging by the space given over to polemics and animated discussions of architectural practice and theory in the professional literature, the Russian architect seems to be much freer in his person and in his thoughts than ever before in his country's history. His opportunities are more numerous, more varied. His horizon has widened and he is ambitious for new conquests. He works harder and his team spirit is enhanced.

BUILDING FOR THE NEW MODE OF LIVING

All building activity in the Soviet Union is intimately bound up with the process of Industrialization, and therefore, the inevitable concomitants of the latter, such as the enormous growth of the urban population, the springing up over night of new industrial centers and towns, have presented new and pressing problems of providing housing accommodations for the armies of workers. Here, because of the ambitious tasks undertaken by the government in the transformation of society, new ground is broken, new vistas in the realm of town planning are opened up, but this is a subject to be discussed at length elsewhere. The inherent characteristics of industrialization, such as the greater employment of women, the premature independence of the young, and the consequent change in the mode of home economics have created special problems for the Soviet architects.

It has been the chief aim of the Soviet architects to develop a type of building that would satisfy the trend towards the collectivization of the utility services and of the economic and housing institutions. The contemplated type is to be suitable to the people's mode of living and their customs and yet leading to the transition from the private kitchen and laundry to the co-operative kitchen, restaurant and laundry, from the private nursery to the co-operative crèche and kindergarden, from the private store and shop to the central government store. They want to develop a type of dwelling that will eliminate housekeeping drudgery from the family and bring about new opportunities and more leisure for cultural activities. The hope is that this will create a bigger demand for new schools, clubs, stadiums and theatres, "all this but a preliminary to that state of collective existence which Engels characterized as the passage from the realm of necessity to the realm of freedom."

There naturally has been much controversy in the Union as to what should be the ideal type of dwelling. Should it take the form of detached single family cottages grouped about a

large green area or should the multiple dwelling type containing individual flats, or the dormitory type prevail? This is
the all important problem of Soviet planning of tomorrow.

Several types have been tried with various degrees of
success. The general tendency is in favor of big housing block-
dwellings providing accommodations for from several hundred to several thousand persons. It is proposed to provide
for every adult absolute privacy for rest and recuperation.[1]
The library and study rooms would be shared in common.
Food storage, kitchen, mess hall, meeting rooms, laundry, the
gymnasium with its appurtenances would be component units
of each block dwelling. The children would be housed according to their age in crèches and kindergardens forming a part
of, or directly attached to this building. It is hoped to attain
in this "house-commune," through the introduction of the
principle of socialization into the individual units, an organic
connection between the individual cells, and the whole complex. Thus a new architectural housing type is to be developed. This type of house-commune has found official ap-
proval, but no satisfactory architectural solution has been
presented thus far. Ingrained habits and customs do not seem
to favor too hasty a change in the manner of living, and the
government is not in too great a hurry to bring about over-
night changes in that direction. Steps are being taken towards
evolving a socialized mode of living, by building enormous
kitchen-factories, restaurants, clubhouses, theatres, colossal
public bathing and laundry establishments, communal clinics,
etc. Much has been done in the realization and development
of the architectural types of these utility services. Their inner
functional workings, and mechanical installations have been
perfected. These communal utility services are beginning to

[1] A room with a minimum floor area of 8.5 square meters.

take the place of the part played by the individual cells in home life, and so, a new collectivist mode of living is gradually being evolved and is supplanting the individualistic mode.

ECONOMICS IN BUILDING MATERIALS

The self-imposed rapid tempo of industrialization of the land by its own means has complicated the problem of the distribution of the available structural materials. The government is forced to allocate them on a priority basis. It has to give practically all of its metal to the building of machinery and tools, all the cement to the construction of dams, various hydro-electric projects, and important industrial enterprises, and therefore, it can give to the construction of housing and communal buildings only secondary materials and left-overs. It is doing much work in the field of technological research, and Soviet architects, in striving for greater economy, are constantly testing and revising the standards of safety. Various sets of standards have been devised by the special commission formed by the Council of Labor and Defense. Research has been carried on with a view to the discovery of new building materials combining lightness, heat-conserving and fire-resisting qualities. Successful experimentation has been carried on with slabs composed of clinkers and diatom earth, slabs of compressed wood shavings (fibrolith), flax by-products, peat, straw and reeds. Out of economy considerations, stringent building codes have been devised. A number of governmental decrees have been promulgated regulating the use of materials, thicknesses of walls and partitions, sizes of windows, etc., forbidding unnecessary protuberances, projections and balconies. The entire basis of its building industry is being energetically reconstructed with the idea of going over to an intensive standardization and mass production system of the structural elements in building, to pre-fabrication processes, the units to be assembled at the desired places. Because of the economic pressure Russian building processes, standards and design have been greatly affected. The simplest and most direct solutions are sought with the result that architecture is often reduced to stark engineering.

NEW FORMS IN DESIGN

In design Russia is venturing upon unusual and significant forms. In the effort to be dialectical the Russian architects are trying to reflect in their work the process of life about them, to mirror the seething activity, the ceaseless movement that are characteristic of Russia's life. Their ambition is to create a dynamic architecture. This dynamic quality is to be stressed not only in single structures but in the composition of whole architectural complexes: streets, settlements and towns. They were experimenting with the juxtaposition of different geometrical forms; cylinders and spheres in conjunction with cubes and parallelepipeds etc. Daring innovation has been shown in the treatment of voids and solids, in the use of sharply conflicting masses and forms. Diversity of directions and contrast in materials are ingeniously handled, lending a dynamic quality to the work. The static architectural forms are reserved for the more monumental type of public buildings: Soviet palaces, libraries, hospitals, houses of rest, etc., but even there they combine and form a unity with the dynamic forms.

The principles of bilateral and axial symmetry or the emphasis on the central part of the composition are regarded as products of a formal aristocratic age, as symbols of the domination of the propertied classes. They are discarded as irrelevant and lifeless. Instead, the asymmetrical schemes of design and the employment of the principle of regularity are preferred. They are used to advantage in accentuating the general interest of the composition and in expressing the function of the structure in a direct manner. Applied ornament is tabooed as unessential and outmoded. In its place, the incidental features of design; details of fenestration, of entrances, wall capping, parapets, railings, lettering, or details symbolic of the underlying structure, provide most of the decoration.

The Soviet architecture of the early thirties bears the unmistakable imprint of the teachings of Le Corbusier, Gropius, Mendelsohn and other modern Western European architects. The Russian laity is apt to refer to that mode as "Soviet style," but in reality there is hardly any trace of anything distinctively Russian about it except its super-seriousness, severity and asceticism. Broadly speaking, it is highly rational, soberly efficient, stripped of all non essentials,—International Functionalism. There is a vigorous freshness about these buildings, a welcome absence of pretense and fuss, and as a result a complete lack of vulgarity. In most cases only fitness and function are relied upon to give the building whatever beauty there is inherent in those qualities.

The positive virtues of this architecture are its freedom from the cramping effect of slavery to old rules, its complete emancipation from traditional clichés, and its unity of thought and feeling in design.

Its shortcomings are its all-too-obvious self-consciousness about function and structure, and its intensive standardization. It is altogether too enthusiastic in its insistence upon expression of the horizontal and vertical elements of the structure. The effects achieved are very often similar to the superstructures of modern liners—long horizontal stripes with a multitude of mullions. Long slits in the wall,—the fenestration idioms of the new mode—are used only too often to accentuate height and vertical continuity. Intensive standardization and the ubiquitous harsh gray color of the buildings lend a certain monotonous aspect to Soviet architecture of those years. This is perhaps excusable on grounds of stringent economy. These buildings do form a striking contrast in their bare and gray simplicity to the colorful and ornate buildings of the pre-Revolutionary period.

Whatever may be said about this "style," it has the virtue of asking from the architect and the builder less than do the historic styles. It does contribute to the speed of building, and it is certainly economical. It marks, as dramatically as possible the complete break between the old Russia and the new.

It seems as though the particular Slavic temperament, which has affected the older Russian architecture, has also affected, though in an entirely different manner, the Russian architecture of the early thirties. In the past, the quality of intensity, so characteristic of the Slav, revealed itself in the sensuous aspects of his architecture. Now, the same intensity reveals itself in a worship of logic and rationalism in building. In their rebellion against the "Bourgeois" past, against its philosophy and its architectural esthetics, the Russians have shown an inclination toward too indiscriminate a denial of "Bourgeois" art, a too zealous, uncritical and literal adoption of the Marxian dialectic in architecture. As a result, much of the building of that period is very little removed from engineering, and it is indeed questionable whether this type of architecture can justifiably claim to have a style at all, in the architectural sense of the word, any more than a business order, however to the point, terse or efficient for its purpose, can lay claim to literature.

The national mentality and the artistic genius which have done so much throughout her history in assimilating, transforming and resolving alien architectural elements into a national substance—those same qualities are unmistakably at work now. The dialectic quality and the highly rationalized work of the present is very much akin to the severe logic and rationalism of the ancient Novgorod and Pskov builders. The spirit of asceticism and frugality which permeates some of the Soviet architecture of today bears a strong resemblance to the simplicity and severity of the architecture of the ancient and free city of "Lord Novgorod."

WHITHER SOVIET ARCHITECTURE?

Architecture in the land of the Soviets is far from having arrived at a definite solution for her many and varied problems. It is still in a debatable stage, full of incongruities and conflicts, doubts and hopes, as Russian life itself. Straddling between a period that is moribund and another period that is still in its infancy, the leaders in architectural thought are groping about for suitable stylistic expressions. They have devised and continue to devise new formulas, new bases for their architectural esthetic, but the question is just how to apply these attractively sounding formulas and theories to the actual practice of architecture.

In recognizing and re-affirming the stand that Lenin took in regard to the accumulated cultural wealth of the past the question arises just which of the great cultures is closest in spirit to the culture which the Soviets are trying to create. Which of the architectural styles of the past could serve as a "point d'appui," as a foundation on which to build the new architecture? This question has been agitating the minds of the

Soviet estheticians for the last several years. The many architectural competitions held in the last few years, especially the
competition for the Palace of the Soviets held in 1931 (the
chief event in the artistic life of the USSR) have focused the
attention of the Soviet architects on this problem.[1] The Palace
of the Soviets is supposed to be, in many ways, the rival and
the antithesis of the Palace of the League of Nations. It is to be
"the architectural monument, the ideological reflection and
practical expression of the chief aims and aspirations of Soviet
Russia." The competition program did not set any definite
style for the building but it did demand "that the monu-
mentality, simplicity, integrity and elegance of the architectural conception of the Palace should reflect the grandeur and
sublimity of Soviet construction."

Here is what Professor Brunov said in regard to the projects
entered in that competition by the Russian architects: "It has
shown that in respect to unity of technique and ideology a
great deal of work remains yet to be done. The utmost sub-
jectivism and the instability of the presented and exhibited
projects proves that the Soviet architects have not yet shown
a distinct type of proletarian architecture." He goes on to say:
"This is comprehensible and explainable, as ideological superstructures usually are late in history. They are always lagging
behind social and economic changes."[2]

It is significant that the Russian architects, B. M. Iofan and
N. B. Joltovsky, who were awarded the first and third places
respectively, have expressed themselves in a language of by-
gone architectural epochs. Iofan, in the words of the official
report: "took from the models of antiquity their unlabored
style, their clarity and simplicity—and that by way or re-work-

---

[1] There were entered 160 architectural projects and 112 separate pro-
posals. Of the architectural projects 136 were submitted by Russian and 24
by foreign architects.
[2] N. Brunov. VOKS. No. 10–12, 1931 Moscow.

ing the elements of the classic ensemble and the models of the old architectural heritage he had tried to arrive at a synthesis of technique and art."

Joltovsky, to quote further "has combined the elements of Classicism with those of the feudal castle: Kremlin towers, enclosed courts, fortress walls, etc." Neither one of these projects was fully acceptable.

As to the project submitted by Mr. Hamilton, (placed second) the Jury found the symmetrical scheme of the plan, the grouping of the principal elements and the distribution of the auditoriums not acceptable. The architectural conception was praised because of its "compactness, simplicity, and fine scale." On the other hand, it was pointed out that "the facades are excessively broken up by the monotonous sameness of the vertical elements. The main approach and the principal elements of the Palace are oriented without regard to the given plot." The plan with its architectural expression (shaping) in relation to the organic function of the Palace was adjudged unsuccessful.[1]

The Jury's remarks pertaining to the project submitted by Le Corbusier throw light on the official attitude towards Ultra-Functionalism. It was admitted to be a master piece of Functionalism. Its bold and clever technico-architectural conception was applauded but the project was dismissed because of a too pronounced cult of Machinism and of esthetization, and because of its poorly articulated primary purpose.[2]

[1] These remarks were gleaned from the Official Report of N. P. Zapletin, Secretary of the Commission of Experts for the Palace of the Soviets' Competition.

[2] The Palace Construction Council found it necessary to order further revisions and developments of the 12 best projects. The winning design was chosen through a two-stage competitive elimination process. B. M. Iofan's project was accepted May 10, 1933, as a working basis. He was appointed chief architect, while the academicians Schouko and Prof. Helfreich were nominated co-workers.

The awards and the critically reasoned comments of the Competition Jury are perhaps the best indication of the direction into which Soviet architecture is drifting. It is evident that the ertswhile infatuation for stark Utilitarianism, naked, engineering and ultra-modern Functionalism is on the wane. Soviet Russia is rejecting them, because their underlying principles are expressive of an age of machine domination over man, a concept contrary to the ultimate aims of the Soviet social theories.

But there are other motives for the rejection of Ultra-Utilitarianism and Functionalism, motives that can be traced to the deeper rhythms and stirrings within her national artistic consciousness. The innate yearning of Russia for a fuller, richer life, for brighter colors, for more warmth is beginning to assert itself. Soviet Russia, in coming of age and in sensing her young strength, is reaching out for the things she has always longed for, things she has had to deny herself all these years. The accumulation of material things has stimulated a desire for an architecture dictated, not entirely, by stringent economy. Her palaces and public buildings must not be just mere efficient machines but must be worthy of her ideals. "They must reflect the grandeur and sublimity of her national construction."

In searching for tangible ideals on which to build her future artistic life, the Soviet theoreticians are critically examining the nature and character of the great artistic epochs and styles. The current, though by far not unanimous, opinion is that the styles that are tinged with mysticism, magic or religion, or that are expressive of feudalistic and capitalistic ideology, cannot serve as a fit inspiration for Soviet architecture. Thus the Egyptian, Babylonian and the other Oriental styles, because of their implied mysticism and magic, are ruled out. The Romanesque because of its feudal connotations, the

Gothic because of its religious aspirations, the Italian Renaissance because of its oligarchic and aristocratic associations are not fit, either. There remains the architecture of the ancient democratic Greek world. It is true, according to A. Lunacharsky (former Soviet Commissar of Education) that those democracies were founded on slavery, but nevertheless they were favorably characterized by Marx because of the freedom and the many-sided accomplishments of the republics' citizenry. Lunacharsky fully takes into consideration the many reasons for the impossibility and incongruity of wholesale transplantation of the Hellenic architectural forms into the USSR. He does not forget the relative climatic differences, the differences in size of the respective republics and the consequent differences in requirements and scale of building: neither does he overlook the wide gap in the methods of construction and character of materials, but he does find in that "cradle of civilization and art" much that is of value, much that is inspirational and that could serve as a guide for the development of the architecture of Russia.[1]

There are other leading estheticians who have expressed a longing for the simplicity, the charm and the gracious democratic qualities of the architecture of Athens. They have gone a step farther and have focused their attention on the heirs of Greece, on the Romans, who have developed the ideals of Greece and incorporated them into the building of vast public utility works. And so it is the spirit of ancient Greece and Rome that is being invoked as an inspiration for a new Proletarian Renaissance,—Athens and Rome re-appraised, re-vitalized and so re-fashioned, so as to fit the purposes and ideals of the young Soviet Republic.

The picture of a Phidias or an Ictinus dressed in Russian blouse and boots may seem grotesque, but the vision of a Ren-

[1] A. Lunacharsky, "Stroitelstvo Moskvy," June 1933.

aissance of Classic antiquity conceived and guided by Soviet estheticians is not as fantastic as it may appear at first glance. It is merely one of those recurrent beats in the pulse of Russia's artistic life, an echo of the great Classic revival of the barely century old Alexandrian period and of the more distant but similarly vital architectural traditions of ancient Novgorod and Pskov.

MOSCOW

СХЕМА ПЛА

SCHEMATIC MASTER PLAN

НИРОВКИ МОСКВЫ

FOR THE CITY OF MOSCOW

PLATE LXX

MONUMENT TO THE THIRD INTERNATIONAL
V. E. Tatlin, 1919.

PLATE LXXI

CLUB HOUSE

Moscow, 1929. I. A. Golossov, architect.

PLATE LXXII

MOSCOW SOVIET BUILDING
Stankevich Street, Moscow, 1930. Academician I. A. Fomin, architect.

Note the novel treatment of double and triple semi-columns, extending through the entire height of the building—a favorite device of Mr. Fomin—for the vertical articulation of his facades.

PLATE LXXIII

Courtesy "Architecture U.S.S.R."

THEATRE, PALACE OF CULTURE
Moscow, 1933. Vesnin Brothers, architects.

The Works of

ACADEMICIAN A. V. SHCHOUSSEV, ARCHITECT

Mr. Shchoussev is a member of the older generation of architects. A great student and admirer of the Russian national heritage, he is one of the most gifted and prolific of his profession—a happy combination of the learned archeologist, practical builder and sensitive artist. He is the designer of the Lenin mausoleum, the Marx-Engels-Lenin Institute at Tbilissi, the Academy of Science in Moscow and many other buildings. In 1941 he was awarded the Stalin Prize, 1st class and named "Laureate of the Stalin Prize."

PLATE LXXIV

Courtesy Sovfoto, N.Y.

THE KAZAN RAILWAY STATION
Moscow, 1913. Academician A. V. Shchoussev, architect.

The construction of the station, begun in 1913, is still going on. When finished, it will be twice
its original size. In designing it, the architect has combined the best national forms of ancient
Russian architecture with those of the Orient, doing it with great understanding and sympathy.
The treatment is highly individual, but the typical characteristics of those forms are faithfully
and lovingly adhered to. Being a great proponent of creative team work, he has from the very
beginning invited some of the best known Russian architects and artists of that period to collaborate with him. Among them were: Benois, Roerich, Koustodiev and Lanceray.

PLATE LXXV

THE LENIN MAUSOLEUM

Moscow, 1926. Academician A. V. Shchoussev, architect.

The design is restrained in character and the general silhouette is suggestive of an ancient burial-mound of some great tribal chief.

The exterior finish is granite, labradorite and porphyry. The dominant colors are red and black, and its simple and serene masses harmonize beautifully with the picturesque ensemble of the Kremlin.

Located on the Red Square at the very wall of the aged Kremlin, the mausoleum was conceived as a tribune from which, on gala or solemn occasions, the marching throngs could be reviewed and addressed.

In the general theme of reconstruction, it is envisioned as the main theme in the composition of the Red-Square ensemble.

PLATE LXXVI   *Courtesy American-Russian Institute, San Francisco*

THE LENIN MAUSOLEUM
Moscow, 1926. Academician A. V. Shchoussev, architect.

The mausoleum, relatively small in scale, is tied in organically with the entire Red Square ensemble and with the walls and towers of the Kremlin. Serene and simple in the form of its masses, it accentuates the dynamic picturesqueness of the medieval castle walls and watch towers.

The Spass Tower (left foreground), over the Saviour's Portal (Spasskia Vorota) of the Kremlin, dates back to 1491. Its lower part was constructed by the Italians M. Rouffo and P. A. Solari. The upper part, richly decorated with Gothic ornament, was added in 1625 by the Englishman Christopher Galloway.

PLATE LXXVII

THE MEYERHOLD THEATRE, PROJECT

Moscow, 1932. Academician A. V. Shchoussev, architect.

The tower is not an organic element of the theatre. It is, more, a part of the general landscape composition of the Mayakovsky Square Ensemble. It is treated as a monumental pedestal for the main sculptural group, symbolic of the theatre. The wall surfaces are decorated with low-relief sculptured panels, groups depicting some of the famous scenes from the various stage productions of this theatre.

PLATE LXXVIII   BUILDING FOR THE COMMISSARIAT OF AGRICULTURE
Moscow, 1933. Academician A. V. Shchoussev, architect.

The design of this building belongs to the "constructivist" phase in the long creative career of this very gifted and prolific architect.
It is a temporary "deflection," as it were, from his lifelong "traditionalism" in architecture.

PLATE LXXIX

HOTEL "MOSCOW"
Moscow, 1935

A. V. Shchusev, O. A. Stapran, architects

PLATE LXXX

THE MARX-ENGELS-LENIN INSTITUTE
Tbilissi, Georgia, 1938. Academician A. V. Shchoussev, architect.

This winning design in a competition of six was awarded the 1941 Stalin prize of the first class (100,000 roubles).

The low-relief sculptured groups in the wing panels, by the Georgian sculptor Nikoladze, depict the revolutionary activities of Stalin.

The sculptured frieze, depicting the various phases of socialist upbuilding in the Caucasus, is by the Georgian sculptor Tamara Abakelia.

PLATE LXXXI   THE U.S.S.R. ACADEMY OF SCIENCES, PROJECT

Main Building, Moscow. Photo from model, 1939.

Academician A. V. Shchoussev, architect.

This building is to house the academy presidium, the main library, and a number of museums and institutes. It is one of a projected very large group of buildings for the various branches of the academy.

PLATE LXXXII

THE U.S.S.R. ACADEMY OF SCIENCES, PROJECT
Conference Hall, Main Building, Moscow
Academician A. V. Shchoussev, architect.

Circular in form with a seating capacity of 1000. The cupola about 120 ft. in diameter is rather
at and is reminiscent of the Roman Pantheon.

PLATE LXXXIII

THE U.S.S.R. ACADEMY OF SCIENCES, PROJECT.
Grand Stairway and Lobby, Main Building, Moscow
A. V. Shchoussev, architect.

PLATE LXXXIV

SPORT PALACE OF THE AVIAKHIM AIRPLANE WORKERS

Moscow, 1934. N. A. Metline, architect.

OFFICE BUILDING FOR THE MINISTRY
OF LIGHT INDUSTRIES

Moscow, 1934. Le Corbusier, architect.

The building contains offices for thirty-five hundred people, a social club with a large auditorium, restaurant and gymnasium.

It embodies many of the characteristic features of Le Corbusier's architecture: huge expanses of glass walls, striking contrasts between the smooth planes of plate glass and those of the rose-colored tuff stone walls, the use of stilts (his beloved "pilotis") for raising the first floor above ground, ramps, curved staircases, and flat roofs.

The building was projected in 1928–29 and the first section erected in 1934. It was received with mixed feelings, and some of the leading architectural theoreticians were inclined to consider it as an already dated stylistic phenomenon, embodying the characteristic tendencies of the architectural thought of the late twenties.

PLATE LXXXV

Courtesy Sovfoto, N.Y.

OFFICE BUILDING FOR THE MINISTRY OF LIGHT INDUSTRIES

PLATE LXXXVI

CLUB FOR TRAMWAY WORKERS
Moscow, 1929. K. C. Melnikov, architect.

PLATE LXXXVII

APARTMENT HOUSE FOR GOVERNMENT EMPLOYEES

North Elevation

Moscow, 1928–1931. B. M. Iofan, architect.

PLATE LXXXVIII

THE TCHAIKOVSKY CONCERT HALL
Formerly The Meyerhold Theatre, Moscow

PLATE LXXXIX

APARTMENT HOUSE
Sadovaya Street, Moscow

PLATE XC

OFFICE BUILDING FOR THE COUNCIL OF PEOPLES COMMISSARS

Okhotny Ryad, Moscow, 1935. A. J. Langman, architect.

PLATE XCI

PASSENGER STATION

Pier at the Khimki Port on the Volga-Moscow Canal
Moscow, 1936. A. M. Roukhliadev, architect.

PLATE XCII   *Courtesy Sovfoto, N.Y.*

THE FRUNZE MILITARY ACADEMY
Moscow, 1936. Academician L. V. Roudnev, architect.

Decorative sculptural details, motifs representing the activities of the various branches of the Red Army, are by the sculptor I. Krestovski.

PLATE XCIII

THE FRUNZE MILITARY ACADEMY
Moscow, 1936
Academician L. V. Roudnev, architect.

Courtesy Sovfoto, N.Y.

PLATE XCIV

THE LENIN STATE LIBRARY

General view, corner Mokhovaya and Komintern Streets, Moscow, 1938

Academician V. A. Schouko and Prof. V. G. Helfreich, architects

The library is one of the principal elements in the general scheme of the Palace of the Soviets Square Ensemble. The architects who, with Academician Iofan, are the co-authors of the Palace have designed the Library with an eye on the huge masses of the coming Palace. They have gauged the formations and the scale of the architectural elements of the library to harmonize with those of the future dominant structure.

PLATE XCV

THE LENIN STATE LIBRARY

Mokhovaya Street elevation, Moscow, 1938

Academician V. A. Schouko and Professor V. G. Helfreich, architects

PLATE XCVI

THE LENIN STATE LIBRARY

Mokhovaya Street elevation, Moscow, 1938

Academician Schouko and Prof. Helfreich, architects; Moukhina, Krandievskaya and Manizer, sculptors
To the left is the "old" Lenin Library, originally known as the "Pashkov House."

PLATE XCVII

THE CENTRAL RED ARMY THEATRE MODEL
Academician K. S. Alabyan, V. N. Simbirtzev, architects

PLATE XCVIII

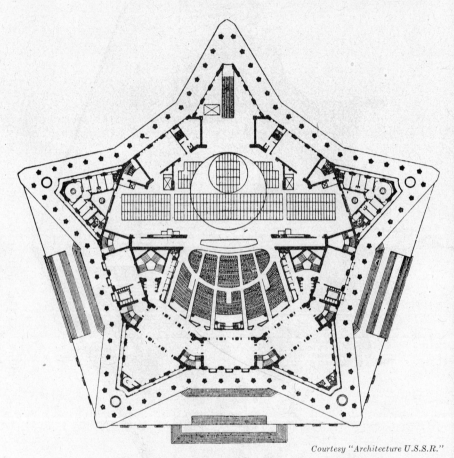

THE CENTRAL RED ARMY THEATRE FLOOR PLAN
Moscow, 1940

Academician K. S. Alabyan, V. N. Simbirtzev, architects.

PLATE XCIX   THE CENTRAL RED ARMY THEATRE

Moscow, 1940. Academician K. S. Alabyan and V. N. Simbirtzev, architects.

The Theatre, monumental in character, was envisioned as the dominant feature in a group of existing and projected Red Army buildings. The architectural conception of the ensemble is Baroque in spirit.

The general plan of the building is in the shape of a five-pointed star, the emblem of the Red Army, but the actual functional elements
of the theatre—the auditorium, the foyer, the stage and all their appurtenances—are contained within a regular decagon, about 300
feet in diameter.

PLATE C   THE CENTRAL RED ARMY THEATRE

Moscow, 1940. Academician K. S. Alabyan and V. N. Simbirtzev, architects.

PLATE CI

MOTION PICTURE THEATRE IN THE PARK AT MALAKHOVKA

Moscow Suburb, 1939

PLATE CII

THE NEW CRIMEAN SUSPENSION BRIDGE
Over the Moscow River
A. V. Vlasov, architect; B. P. Konstantinov, engineer.

Total length, including approaches, approx........ 2400 ft.
Main Span .... 550 ft.

PLATE CIII   CENTRAL POSTAL, TELEPHONE AND TELEGRAPH BUILDING
Moscow, circa 1936

PLATE CIV

Courtesy American-Russian Institute, San Francisco

APARTMENT HOUSE FOR EMPLOYEES OF METROSTROI
Sokolniki Street, Moscow, 1937

PLATE CV

APARTMENT HOUSE

FOR MEMBERS OF THE INSTITUTE OF STATE PLANNING COMMISSION

Moscow

PLATE CVI

APARTMENT BUILDINGS
"Avenue of the Enthusiasts," Moscow

PLATE CVII

THE KAPITSA INSTITUTE FOR PHYSICAL RESEARCH

Lenin Hills, Moscow

PLATE CVIII

HOUSE AT KOSTINO
Moscow Suburb

Design for window shutter. Note the revival of the pictorial idioms of old rural Russia.

PLATE CIX

APARTMENT BUILDINGS

AT THE TEXTILE MANUFACTURING CENTER

Ivanovo, 1939

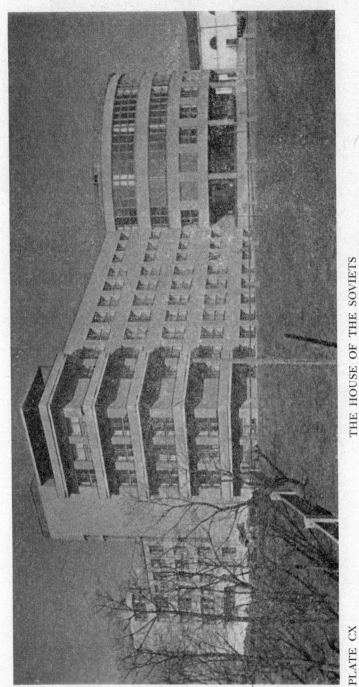

THE HOUSE OF THE SOVIETS
Gorki, 1931. A. Z. Greenberg, architect.

PLATE CX

The Moscow Subway

PREFACE TO THE PLATES

THE MOSCOW SUBWAY

IT IS, PERHAPS, with pardonable pride that the Russians point to their Subway not only as the safest and the most comfortable in the world, but as the most "elegant and the most beautiful in the world." The extravagant splendor of the whole system and the individual elegance of the stations have been seized upon again and again by various Soviet officials to indicate to the outside world the great artistic success realized under the patronage of the State.

The architectural characteristics of the group of structures, comprising the entrance pavilions and subterranean elements of the Moscow Subway (or The Metro as the Russians call it), are indicative of the processes that have been taking place in the development of Soviet architecture. They clarify and confirm certain tendencies that have become noticeable in the decade.

As the reader will notice, there are represented several stylistic tendencies, ranging from the "classical" to the "modern." Indeed, there are quite a few cases where the surface and sub-surface elements were designed by representatives of diverse architectural persuasions, differing considerably in conception and approach to "style." However, there is one great unifying element in the conception of the entire system. It is the unity of artistic purpose, the unity of effort to glamorize and dramatize the architectural elements and features of this underground railway, to make it a symbol of a fine culture, a promise of a gracious and easier life to come.

It was not enough to make it, as the Russians claim it to be, the safest, most efficient and most comfortable in the world, but it had to be the most beautiful, luxurious and sumptuous of its kind. It seems as though Soviet Russia has gone out all the way to lavish upon the Subway of its capital city all the skill and ingenuity of its engineers, the wealth and substance of its natural resources, and the imaginative power and artistry of its architects.

One of the main reasons for this outpouring of great effort and material wealth was the fact that the subway system was conceived as an integral part of the very ambitious program for the replanning, reconstruction and beautification of Moscow. It was to be an extension, as it were, of the city's beautification program carried on from its avenues and boulevards to the underground concourses, foyers and train platforms of the subway.

СХЕМА ЛИНИЙ 1-ой ОЧЕР
МОСКОВСКОГО МЕТРОПОЛИТ

СТ. ОХОТНЫЙ РЯД

СТ. АРБАТСКАЯ ПЛ.

МЕТРО
СТ. СМОЛЕНСКАЯ ПЛ.

МЕТРО
СТ. БИБ. ЛЕНИНА

СТ.

СТ. ДВОРЕЦ СОВЕТОВ

СТ. КРЫМСКАЯ ПЛ.

KEY

First Section of the

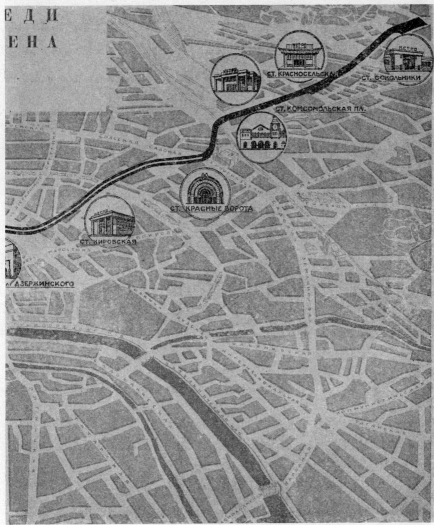

Courtesy "Stroitelstvo Moskvy"

PLAN
Moscow Subway

PLATE CXI

Courtesy American-Russian Institute, San Francisco

THE SOKOLNIKI STATION ENTRANCE PAVILION
Moscow, 1934. Bikova and Taranov, architects.

Manizer and Mitkovitzer, sculptors.

The Station, the very first of the series, is located on an avenue leading to Sokol-niki Park Circle. It is designed to serve a dual purpose, that of Park Portal and Subway entrance. The sculptured frieze, accentuating the entrance, is based on a theme symbolizing the various stages of the subway (Metro) construction. The physical culture theme of the statues is in keeping with the general character of the park activities.

(By the way, it might be noted that Miss Bikova is one of the younger generation of successful women architects. She is also the co-designer of the Byelorussian Station.)

PLATE CXII

Courtesy Sovfoto, N.Y.

THE SOKOLNIKI STATION TRANSFER CORRIDOR
Moscow, 1934. Bikova and Taranov, architects.

PLATE CXIII

SOKOLNIKI STATION UNDERGROUND PLATFORM
Moscow, 1934. Bikova and Taranov, architects.

One of the 13 underground stations, comprising the first section of the
Moscow subway, (the Metro).

PLATE CXIV

LENIN LIBRARY STATION ENTRANCE PAVILION
Moscow, 1934. S. Kravets and I. Kostenko, architects.

SMOLENSKY SQUARE STATION ENTRANCE PAVILION No. 1
Moscow, 1934. S. Andriyevski, architect.

PLATE CXV

SMOLENSKY SQUARE STATION ENTRANCE PAVILION No. 2
Moscow, 1934. S. Andriyevski, architect.

PLATE CXVI

THE CRIMEAN SQUARE STATION ENTRANCE PAVILION

Moscow, 1934. Krutikov, Popov and Andriyevski, architects.

PLATE CXVII   THE PALACE OF THE SOVIETS STATION ENTRANCE PAVILION

Moscow, 1934. Kravetz and Trenke, architects.

Located at the foot of a boulevard the pavilion was conceived as an element of a Park-boulevard ensemble, to serve as Subway Station entrance and boulevard portal.

PLATE CXVIII

Courtesy Sovfoto, N.Y.

THE ARBAT SQUARE STATION ENTRANCE PAVILION
Moscow, 1934. L. Teplitzki, architect.

The plan of the pavilion is in the form of a five pointed star, suggestive of its
nearness to the commissariat of defense building.

PLATE CXIX

THE KURSK RAILWAY STATION DISTRIBUTION HALL

I. S. Teplitzky, architect

PLATE CXX

Courtesy American-Russian Intitute, San Francisco

RED GATES STATION CENTRAL DISTRIBUTION HALL

Moscow, 1934. Academician I. A. Fomin, architect.

The massive piers are lined with dark red highly-polished Caucasian marble "Shrosha." The white vaulted and coffered ceiling is brilliantly lighted. By contrast, it accentuates the deep tones of the columns and produces an effect of spaciousness and height.

The architect, one of the older generation of traditionalists, has utilized the classic forms of design and succeeded in creating a series of very impressive interiors and almost theatrically effective vistas.

PLATE CXXI

Photo Markov; Courtesy Sovfoto, N.Y.

RED GATES STATION ENTRANCE
Moscow, 1934. N. Ladovski, architect.

OKHOTNY RYAD STATION CENTRAL HALL
Moscow, 1934. Borov, Zamski and Revkovski, architects.

PLATE CXXII

THE IZMAILOVSKAYA STATION TRAIN PLATFORM
Moscow, 1944

PLATE CXXIII   THE KOMSOMOL SQUARE STATION SOUTH VESTIBULE DISTRIBUTION HALL

Moscow, 1934. D. H. Tchetchoulin, architect.

The design of the underground halls, lobbies and platforms was awarded the 1941 Stalin Prize, 1st class (100,000 Roubles) and the title "Stalin Prize Laureate" conferred upon the architect.

It was singled out and praised by the Prize Award Committee "because of the vigor and vitality of the general composition, because of the tasteful and great variety of decorative detail, as displayed in the texture and color of the facing materials, and the admirable tile work, the bronze fixtures and the many other felicities."

PLATE CXXIV

Courtesy American-Russian Institute, San Francisco

THE AIRPORT STATION TRAIN PLATFORM
Moscow, 1938. B. S. Vilensky, architect.

PLATE CXXV   THE REVOLUTIONARY SQUARE STATION CENTRAL HALL
Moscow, 1938. A. N. Doushkin, architect.

One of the underground stations of the second section of the Moscow Subway. The monumental high-relief figures at the base of the

PLATE CXXVI

THE DYNAMO STATION ENTRANCE PAVILION

Moscow, 1938. Likhtenberg and Revkovsky, architects.

Leningrad

THE KIROV REGIONAL SOVIET BUILDING
Leningrad, 1935. N. Trotzky, architect.

"Leningrad," Iskoustvo, 1943

MAP OF ST. PETERSBURG AS OF 1911

PLATE CXXVII

"Leningrad," Iskoustvo, 1948

A TECHNICAL SCHOOL

Leningrad, 1936–1937. L. Galeprin and A. Knyazev, architects.

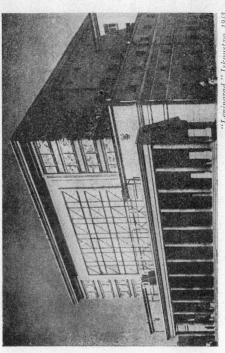

"Leningrad," Iskoustvo, 1948

THE CINEMA "GIANT"

Leningrad, 1936 A. Gegello and D. Krichevsky, architects.

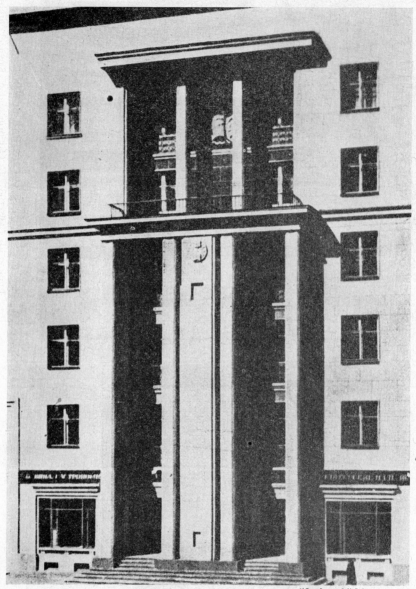

PLATE CXXVIII

"Leningrad," Iskoustvo, 1943

ENTRANCE TO AN APARTMENT HOUSE
Leningrad, 1939–1941. E. Levinson, I. Fomin, and S. Evdokimov, architects.

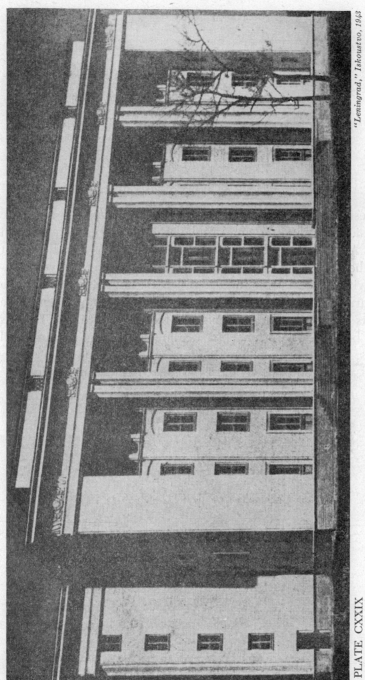

"Leningrad," Iskoustvo, 1943

THE VOLODARSKY REGIONAL SOVIET BUILDING
Leningrad, 1938–1940. E. Levinson and I. Fomin, architects.

PLATE CXXIX

THE HOUSE OF THE SOVIETS

Leningrad. N. Trotzky, architect.

The design of this building (one of his last works), is a sincere expression of this gifted and prolific architect's credo (he died in 1941). A product of the Leningrad Academy of Arts and brought up in the classic tradition, he nevertheless experimented very daringly with the various mutations of "modernism." At one time he was carried away by Constructivism, but somehow even those projects had a romantic and sensuous feeling about them. He was at his best and happiest when dealing with large monumental themes, and expressing himself (to quote him freely) "in a full-bodied, deeply impressive and expressive architectural style."

PLATE CXXX

THE HOUSE OF THE SOVIETS

Main Facade, Leningrad, 1936–1941

N. Trotzky, architect; N. Tomsky, sculptor.

PLATE CXXXI

SCHOOL PROJECT

Leningrad, 1935. N. Trotzky, architect.

PLATE CXXXII

THE HOUSE OF THE KIROV REGIONAL SOVIET
Leningrad, 1935. N. Trotzky, architect.

MISCELLANEOUS
Soviet Republics

THE GOSPROM BUILDINGS ENSEMBLE
Dzerjinski Square, Kharkov

This group of buildings occupies three city blocks, and houses the offices of more than 30 various industries. There are included, for common use, an assembly hall, a library, bank and other functional services. The bridge-like connecting elements, at the upper levels, are a part of a very ingenious intercommunication system.

The competition held for this project was by invitation only, and it did not include Mr. Seraphimov. However, he submitted a project, signing it "An Uninvited Guest." The jury found it to be the most noteworthy and awarded it the first prize.

PLATE CXXXIII

THE HOUSE OF STATE INDUSTRY (GOSPROM)

Birdseye View, Dzerjinski Square, Kharkov, 1925–1929

Prof. S. S. Seraphimov and S. M. Kravetz, architects

The open circular area in front of the group was designed without the architect's collaboration. It is not large enough, in scale, to permit a full appreciation of the group composition as a whole.

PLATE CXXXIV

THE HOUSE OF STATE INDUSTRY (GOSPROM)

Dzerjinski Square, Kharkov, 1925–1929

Prof. S. S. Seraphimov (1878–1939), S. M. Kravetz, architects

PLATE CXXXV

THE HOUSE OF PROJECTS
Dzerjinski Square, Kharkov, 1930
Prof. S. S. Seraphimov and Zandberg, architects

The general architectural style of the State Industry group (right) is also adopted for this structure, thus achieving unity of design in the entire ensemble.

PLATE CXXXVI

HOTEL

Dzerjinski Square, Kharkov, 1933. G. A. Ianovitski, architect.

The general ensemble of the Square was taken into consideration by the architect. The mass silhouette of the hotel, right center, was designed to serve as transitional step between the tall monumental group of the "House of State Industry" (not shown on this photo) and the lower structures on the Liebknecht Street.

PLATE CXXXVII

TURBINE GENERATOR PLANT

BUILDING No. 150 (PROJECT)

Kharkov

PLATE CXXXVIII   KRIVOI ROG METALLURGICAL PLANT STORES AND APARTMENT BUILDINGS

Krivoi Rog, Ukraine, 1935

PLATE CXXXIX

Courtesy Sovfoto, N.Y.

THE LENIN MUSEUM
Kiev, Ukraine, S.S.R.

PLATE CXL   THE BUILDING OF THE COUNCIL OF PEOPLES COMMISSARS
OF THE UKRAINIAN S.S.R.

Kiev, 1937. Academician I. A. Fomin, P. W. Abrossimov, architects.

This detail of the central part of the main facade reveals the highly individual approach of Mr. Fomin to the design of large public buildings and the treatment of the classic order in utilizing it as a means of vertical articulation of his facades.

PLATE CXLI

PROPOSED ENSEMBLE OF SQUARE AND BUILDINGS
ON THE BANKS OF THE DNIEPER RIVER
Novoe Zaporozhye, Ukraine, 1937

Varentsov, Lavrov and Milovanov, architects, under the direction of G. Orlov, architect.

PLATE CXLII.   BUILDING FOR THE SUPREME SOVIET

Kiev, Ukrainian S.S.R., 1939. V. I. Zabolotni, architect.

The architect was awarded the 1941 Stalin Prize, 1st class (100,000 Roubles) and the title "Stalin Prize Laureate" conferred upon him. The building is located on hilly ground, in a park overlooking the river Dnieper. It was singled out and praised by the prize award committee because of the "simplicity and clarity of plan, harmoniousness of architectural forms, well-studied fine scale, and unostentatious detail—qualities which give it warmth, attractiveness and make it expressive of a democratic spirit."

PLATE CXLIII

MOTION PICTURE THEATRE ENTRANCE DETAIL
Stalino, 1939

PLATE CXLIV

Courtesy Sovfoto, N.Y.

RED ARMY HOUSE
Samara (on the Volga), 1932

THE LENIN LIBRARY
Minsk, 1933

PLATE CXLV

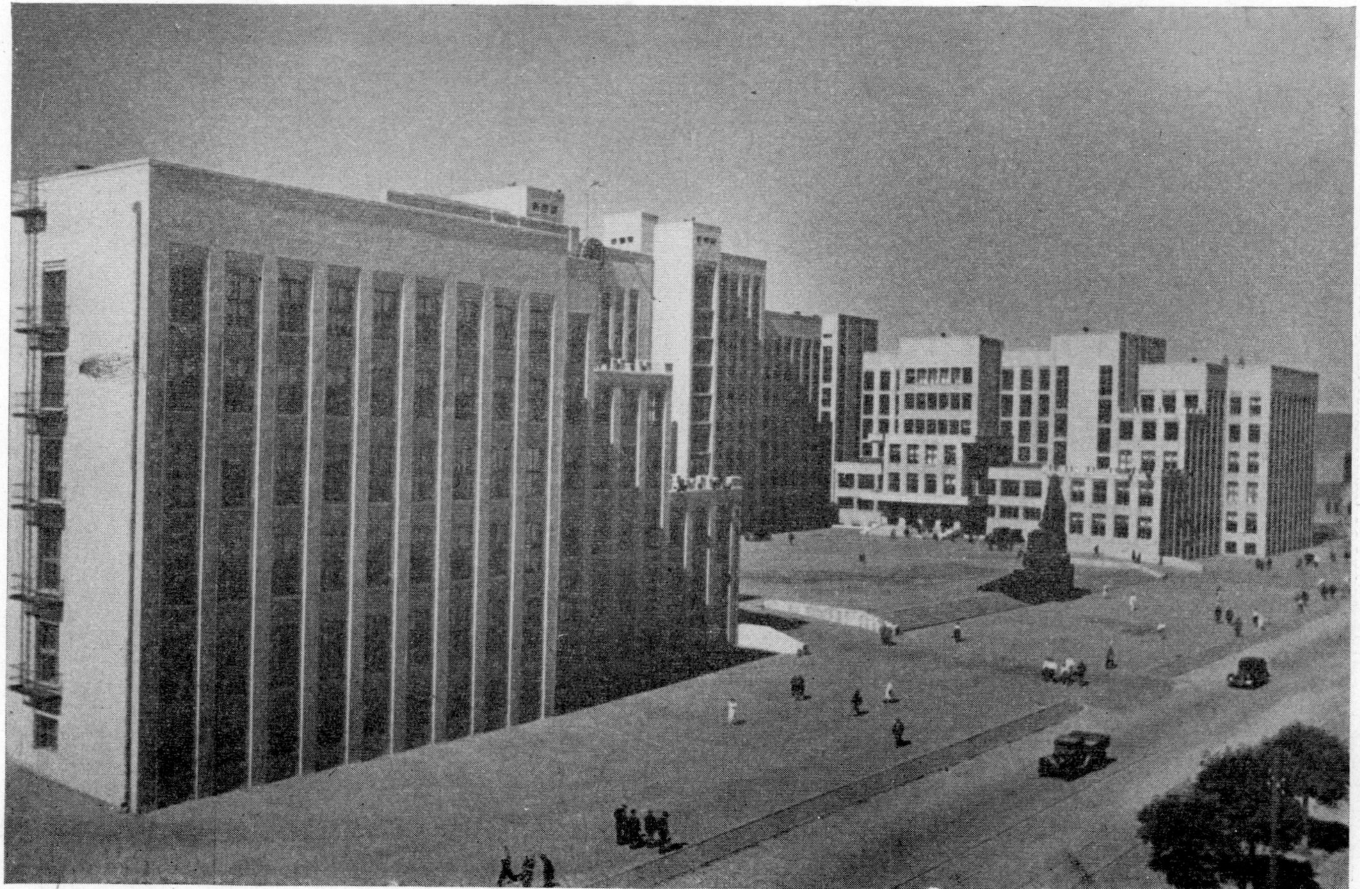

Courtesy American-Russian Institute, San Francisco

PLATE CXLVI

THE GOVERNMENT HOUSE

Minsk, Byelorussia, 1933. I. G. Langbard, architect

PLATE CXLVII

THE RED ARMY BUILDING

Minsk, 1937. I. G. Langbard, architect.

PLATE CXLVIII

THE GOVERNMENT HOUSE

Roustavelli Avenue elevation. Tbilissi, Georgia, 1938.

Professor V. D. Kokorin, architect, in collaboration with G. Lejava

The building is only partly finished. What appears to be the main facade is, in reality, a view of an open court, which is to be

PLATE CXLIX

COMMUNICATIONS BUILDING
Tbilisi, Georgia S. S. R., 1938

PLATE CL

GOVERNMENT PALACE ENTRANCE DETAIL
Tbilisi, Georgia S.S.R., 1938

PLATE CLI

APARTMENT HOUSE
Tbilisi, Georgia S.S.R., 1947

PLATE CLII

THE PEDAGOGICAL INSTITUTE

Stalinabad, Tadzhik S.S.R., 1940

PLATE CLIII

MUNICIPAL BANK ENTRANCE DETAIL
Stalinabad, Tadzhikistan, 1939

PLATE CLIV

STREET IN SVERDLOVSK

(Ural Area—the old and the very new in Architecture)

PLATE CLV

THE URAL BRANCH OF THE ACADEMY OF SCIENCES

To Be Erected at Sverdlovsk

Photo from model, 1939. Gajnutdinov, architect.

Prize winning project in All-Union competition

PLATE CLVI

UNIVERSITY CITY PROJECT
Kazakh State University, Alma Ata

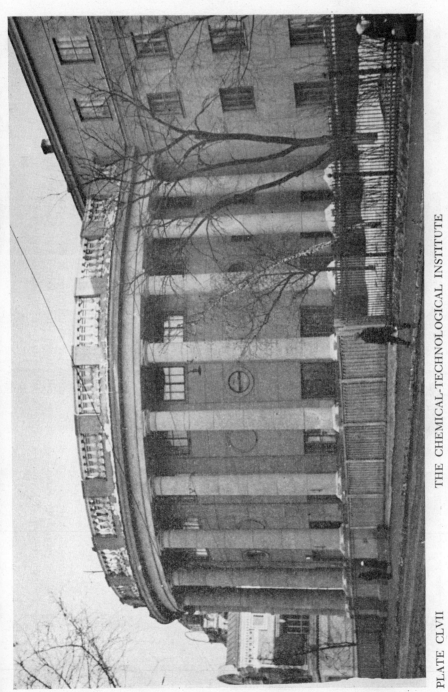

PLATE CLVII   THE CHEMICAL-TECHNOLOGICAL INSTITUTE

Kazan, 1939. Gajnutdinov, architect.

Courtesy Sovfoto, N.Y.

PLATE CLVIII   SANATORIUM OF THE COMMISSARIAT OF HEAVY INDUSTRIES

Sochi, Caucasus. I. S. Kousnetzov, architect.

The Facade of the Sanatorium club house and the main stairway are an indication of the pompous magnificence and the excesses of decorative elements. The entire large ensemble—exteriors and interiors—is overloaded with sumptuous detail. By contrast, the Sanatorium group at Kislovodsk for the same commissariat is designed in a much more rational and simpler manner.

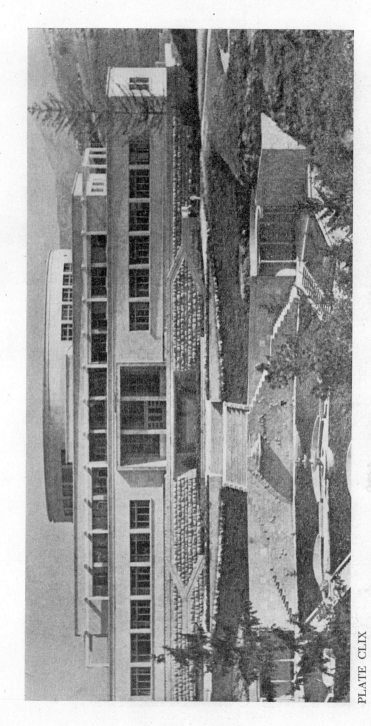

PLATE CLIX

SANATORIUM FOR THE EMPLOYEES OF THE COMMISSARIAT OF HEAVY INDUSTRY

Kislovodsk. M. I. Ginsburg, architect.

SANATORIUM DINING PAVILION
Sochi (on the Black Sea), 1938

PLATE CLX

THE ARAZINDA SANATORIUM
Abastuman, Georgia

PLATE CLXI

PLATE CLXII

HEALTH RESORT HOTEL AT KEMERI
Latvia S.S.R., 1945

The Palace of the Soviets
Moscow

PREFACE TO THE PLATES

THE PALACE OF THE SOVIETS, MOSCOW

THE PROJECT, as submitted by Mr. Iofan [1] in competition with many others, was officially accepted as a basis for further development. It has since undergone careful study and several modifications. The second series of preliminary studies—prepared by Mr. Iofan and the two newly appointed co-authors, Professor Helfreich and Academician Schouko—were approved by the Soviet construction committee in February 1934. The working drawings were completed in March 1937.

In general, the basic concept of the palace design has not undergone any fundamental change. The latest studies reveal a further refinement in the proportions and interrelations of the principal masses, a more vigorous approach to detail, and great improvement in scale.

The height of the Statue of Lenin was increased from 75 meters to 100 meters. The number of the main cylindrical tiers has been decreased from five to three, thus consolidating the principal masses, changing somewhat the original silhouette and the relation of the cylindrical superstructure to the bulk of the base. (See models of 1934 and 1937.)

The principal elements of the palace are: a huge Statue of Lenin (325 feet high), a pedestal—superstructure composed of three receding tiers of cylindrical masses (housing several museums), and an enormous substructure (sort of a stylobate), housing the main and secondary auditoriums. The

[1] Mr. B. M. Iofan (now Academician Iofan), one of the younger members of the profession, will be remembered here as the co-designer of the Soviet pavilion at the New York International Exposition of 1939; also as the designer of the Soviet pavilion at the Paris International Exposition of 1937.

He is a graduate of the Odessa Art School and later on, studied architecture at the Art Institute in Rome.

lower and underground stories are given over to traffic handling, storage, and the complex technical equipment.

The main auditorium (intended for meetings of Congresses and large conventions) has a seating capacity of 20,000. It is designed as a circular amphitheatre (400 ft. dia. and 325 ft. high) with 51 rows of seats. The delegates' seats are arranged on a special movable platform in the center of the arena. When necessary, the platform can be lowered into a pit and the arena space (about 65 ft. in dia.) can be utilized for staging pageants, massed physical culture performances or sport activities. The presidium occupies a section of the amphitheatre's periphery with seats arranged on stepped terraces. The speaker's tribune is located just below the presidium seats. The auditorium is ringed by a circular foyer, connecting with a number of auxiliary halls, vestibules and stairways.

The small auditorium (intended for minor conventions, conferences, theatre performances and concerts) has a seating capacity of 6,000. It is designed as a semicircular amphitheatre with a shallow balcony, a large stage and all the necessary auxiliary appurtenances. A part of this small auditorium unit is a 500,000 volume library, a number of reading and study rooms and four smaller assembly halls.

The rooms for members of the presidium, the government, the diplomatic corps and the press are common to both: the large and small auditoriums. They all have their own entrances, vestibules, dressing rooms and private studies.

PLATE CLXIII   *Courtesy Sovfoto, N. Y.*

THE PALACE OF THE SOVIETS
North West view. Photo from model (as of 1937).

Professor V. G. Helfreich, Academicians B. M. Iofan and V. A. Schouko, architects
Note the vertically articulated and progressively attenuated tiers of cylindrical masses, superimposed upon the storied and terraced stylobate. The designers were striving to give the huge structure a quality of lightness and suppleness, and to achieve a cumulative effect of upward soaring.

The projected structure, judging by published data, is supposed to top every known building in the world. Its height, including the statue, is 419 meters (about 1365 feet). Total cubic contents 6.5 million cubic meters. Total useful floor area about 186.000 square meters.

PLATE CLXIV

PALACE OF THE SOVIETS
North West view. Model as of 1937.

Professor V. G. Helfreich, Academicians B. M. Iofan and V. A. Schouko, architects
On the wall (dimly seen) are the floor plans.

PLATE CLXV   *Courtesy Sovfoto, N. Y.*

THE PALACE OF THE SOVIETS
Main (North) Facade facing the Kremlin. Model as of 1934.

Professor V. G. Helfreich, Academicians B. M. Iofan and V. A. Schouko, architects

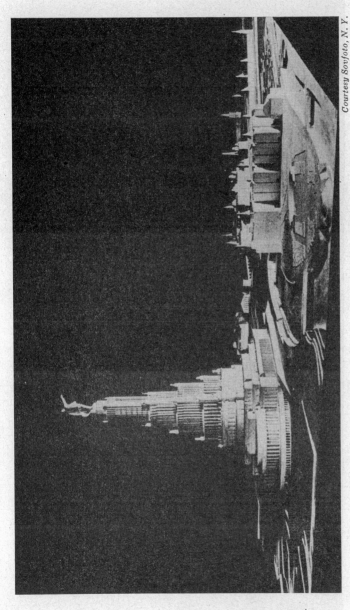

Courtesy Sovfoto, N. Y.

PLATE CLXVI

THE PALACE OF THE SOVIETS

South East view. Model as of 1934.

Professor V. G. Helfreich, Academicians B. M. Iofan and V. A. Schouko, architects

The semi-circular part of the sub-structure houses the small auditorium. In the background to the right is the model of the Kremlin.

PLATE CLXVII

PALACE OF THE SOVIETS

Model of the dominant structure and the neighboring buildings.

Professor V. G. Helfreich, Academicians B. M. Iofan and V. A. Schouko, architects

A skyline study of the palace as seen from the North-East. The Kremlin is in the center foreground.

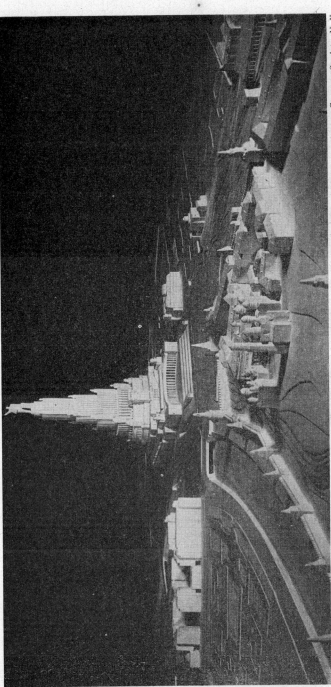

PLATE CLXVIII   THE PALACE OF THE SOVIETS AND THE NEIGHBORING BUILDINGS

North East view. Photo from model (as of 1934).

Professor V. G. Helfreich, Academicians B. M. Iofan and V. A. Schouko, architects

Photo shows relation of the dominant structure to part of the Kremlin ensemble (in the foreground) and to the buildings right and left. The Moscow river flows past the South East wall of the palace, and the South wall of the Kremlin enclosure. Note that the main axis of the palace runs practically parallel with the West wall of the Kremlin and, therefore there will be an unobstructed view of the main facade, along the reconstructed avenue, for approximately one mile.

PLATE CLXIX

THE PALACE OF THE SOVIETS

General Perspective looking North East

Proposed development of the area, enclosed within the Moscow river bend, South South West of the palace.

PLATE CLXX

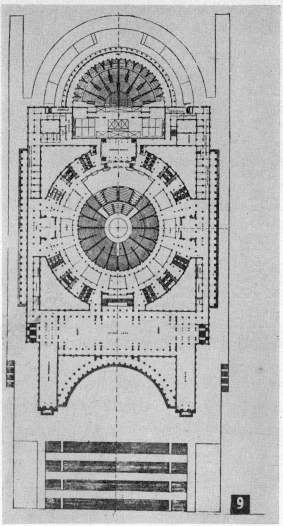

Courtesy "Stroitelstvo Moskvy"

PALACE OF THE SOVIETS
1934 Plan (at the Level of 21 meters)
Helfreich, Iofan and Schouko, architects.

PLATE CLXXI

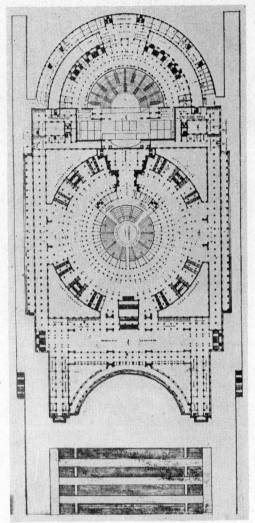

PALACE OF THE SOVIETS
1934 Plan (at the Level of 37.5 meters)
Helfreich, Iofan and Schouko, architects.

PLATE CLXXII

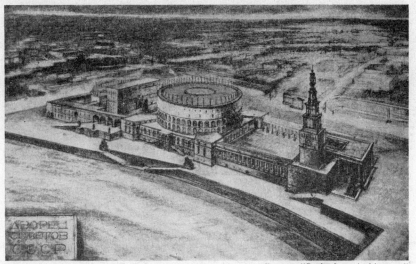

PALACE OF THE SOVIETS
Competition Project, 1932. I. W. Joltovski, architect.
Placed third in competition.

PLATE CLXXIII

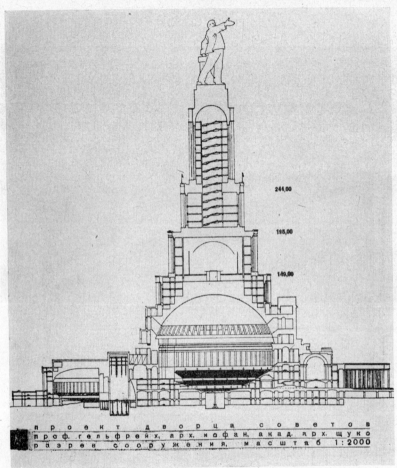

244.00

195.00

149.00

PALACE OF THE SOVIETS
Section, (Winning Project), 1934.
Helfreich, Iofan and Schouko, architects

PLATE CLXXIV

Courtesy "Stroitelstvo Moskvy"

PALACE OF THE SOVIETS
Winning Project (in an International Competition)
Photo from model, February, 1934
Prof. B. G. Helfreich, B. M. Iofan, Academician B. A. Schouko, architects

PLATE CLXXV

PALACE OF THE SOVIETS
Perspective, Competition Project, 1932
H. O. Hamilton, architect

Mr. Hamilton of East Orange, N. J. shared the first prize in the international competition with two Russian architects.

PLATE CLXXVI

PALACE OF THE SOVIETS

Elevation, Competition Project, 1932

H. O. Hamilton, architect

The All-Union Agricultural Exposition
Moscow, 1939–1940

PREFACE TO THE PLATES

ALL-UNION AGRICULTURAL EXPOSITION

THE ALL-UNION AGRICULTURAL EXPOSITION held in Moscow just prior to the war (1939–1940) was, figuratively speaking, a grand parade, at the capital fair, of the many sister republics and their various peoples—all of them displaying their diverse characteristics, bringing their personal artistic contribution to the union, and telling their story in the language of their own national art.

In a practical way it furnished much information about existing rural conditions in the various far-flung republics. It helped to develop farm building types best suited to the specific needs of the many lands and climes of the union.

Artistically, the exposition revealed the wealth and variety of cultures and art-forms of the participating exhibitors. It focused the attention of the Soviet architects and artists on the great monuments of the Transcaucasian and Central-Asiatic republics, on the beauty and charm of the plastic and pictorial arts of the minor nationalities, and the handicrafts of the formerly nomadic tribes.

It was a challenge and, at the same time, a unique opportunity for the Soviet architect to display his talents and ingenuity in adapting this old and rich vocabulary for his uses, analyzing its true significance, developing it, sometimes stylizing it and heightening its characteristics.

Judging by results accomplished, it was done, in many of the pavilions, with great understanding, insight and sympathy.

282

PLATE CLXXVII

Courtesy American-Russian Institute, San Francisco

THE KARELIAN-FINNISH PAVILION
at the All-Union Agricultural Exposition, Moscow, 1939–1940

THE UZBEK PAVILION

at the All-Union Agricultural Exposition, Moscow, 1939–1940

S. N. Poloupanov, architect

Sculpture by Manouilov and Altoukhov

Carving and ornamentation by the Uzbekian craftsmen,
M. Akhmedov and N. Nouroullo.

This is perhaps one of the loveliest and most fascinating of the group. The pavilion is, certainly, not a copy of any of Uzbekian national art monuments. It is rather an inspired architectural conception of a folk theme and its variations, a distillation, as it were, of the more significant art forms, characteristic patterns and rhythms.

Rich and beautiful are the plaster-of-Paris ornaments, arranged in huge circles on the walls. The colored glazed tile lining of the central portal, with its interlacing flower design motives, reminds one of a gorgeous oriental rug. But most striking is the gay rotunda over the pool, with its slender columns, reticular and airy entablature, and its overhanging star-shaped cornice.

The sum-total impression is evocative of a large, gaily appointed, country house of gracious living and hospitality. It somehow makes you feel that this is a corner of Uzbekistan, a part of the sunny landscape and its people.

PLATE CLXXVIII

BIRD'S-EYE VIEW OF THE UZBEK PAVILION
at the All-Union Agricultural Exposition, Moscow, 1939–1940
S. N. Poloupanov, architect

Note the treatment of the wing portals and the rug like design mosaics of the court pavement.

PLATE CLXXIX

Courtesy American-Russian Institute, San Francisco

THE KIRGHIZ PAVILION
at the All-Union Agricultural Exposition, Moscow, 1939–1940
A. Plotnikov, architect

Carved wood, against a background of painted plaster is used very extensively and effectively. The slender, candlestick-like, columns, the entablature, the latticed frames around the niches, they are all richly carved. The characteristic national architectural and decorative forms have been recreated and incorporated successfully. Much of the ornament has been borrowed from the Kirghiz rugs known as the "Toushkeez."

PLATE CLXXX   *Courtesy American-Russian Institute, San Francisco*

THE GEORGIAN PAVILION
at the All-Union Agricultural Exposition, Moscow, 1939–1940
A. G. Kourdiani, architect, awarded the Stalin Prize 2nd Class (50,000 Roubles)

The National forms are adhered to but used in a novel way. Note the clusters of slender columns, narrowing at the base and tied at the top with light arcades—the beloved "atectonic" forms of medieval Georgia—utilized in this case "architectonically" as supporting elements of the structure.

Courtesy American-Russian Institute, San Francisco

THE GEORGIAN PAVILION
Another view. To the right are the Armenian and the Azerbaidjan pavilions.

PLATE CLXXXI

THE KAZAKH PAVILION
at the All-Union Agricultural Exposition, Moscow, 1939–1940
I. Bezroukov, architect

THE KARA-KALPAKIAN PAVILION
at the All-Union Agricultural Exposition, Moscow, 1939–1940
Detail of interior.

PLATE CLXXXII

THE UKRAINIAN PAVILION

at the All-Union Agricultural Exposition, Moscow, 1939–1940

A. Tatzii and I. Ivantchenko, architects

Note the absence of arcades, colonnades and porticoes, so prevalent in many of the other pavilions. Instead, the architects have utilized fluted forms and huge golden cereal spikes for their basic decorative motifs. The entrance arch, richly ornamented, is the one prominent architectural feature accentuating the principal facade.

PLATE CLXXXIII

Courtesy Sovfoto, N. Y.

THE UKRAINIAN PAVILION
at the All-Union Agricultural Exposition, Moscow, 1939–1940
A. Tatzïï, N. Ivantchenko, architects.

PLATE CLXXXIV   *Courtesy American-Russian Institute, San Francisco*

THE TADZHIK PAVILION
at the All-Union Agricultural Exposition, Moscow, 1939–1940
A. Antonenko, M. Zakharov, architects; A. Lavinsky, sculptor

The pavilion has a sprucely dressed-up appearance. Some of the details, especially the open-work ornament, the grilles, are of extraordinary interest.

Courtesy American-Russian Institute, San Francisco

THE MEAT PACKING INDUSTRY PAVILION
at the All-Union Agricultural Exposition, Moscow, 1939–1940

PLATE CLXXXV

THE CENTRAL REGIONS PAVILION
(Kalinin, Smolensk, Orel, Yaroslavl and Ivanov)
at the All-Union Agricultural Exposition, Moscow, 1939–1940
A. V. Kourovski, architect

KURSK, VORONEZH AND TAMBOV REGIONS PAVILION
at the All-Union Agricultural Exposition, Moscow, 1939–1940

PLATE CLXXXVI

THE TADZHIK PAVILION
at the All-Union Agricultural Exposition, Moscow, 1939–1940
A. Antonenko, M. Zakharov, architects
Detail of interior

PLATE CLXXXVII   *Courtesy American-Russian Institute, San Francisco*

THE AZERBAIDJAN PAVILION
S. A. Dadachev and M. A. Ousseinov, architects; Sadije, sculptor
Entrance detail and statue symbolizing the Kolkhoz worker.

PLATE CLXXXIII

THE VETERINARY PAVILION
at the All-Union Agricultural Exposition, Moscow, 1939–1940

PLATE CLXXXIX

THE BYELORUSSIAN PAVILION
at the All-Union Agricultural Exposition, Moscow, 1939–1940
V. Simbirtzev, B. Barkhin, architects; Orlov, sculptor

The ornament of the decorative wall band is derived from national embroidery motifs.